DISCOURSE

THE BASICS

Humans are social animals and are constantly interacting with each other through conversation, written communication, symbols and other expressions. *Discourse: The Basics* is an accessible and engaging introduction to the analysis of those interactions and the many forms and meanings they can take. The book draws on a range of international case studies and examples from literature, political speech, advertising and newspaper articles to address key questions such as:

- What is discourse?
- Why are there different approaches to understanding discourse?
- How are individual interactions connected with the larger discourses that frame our ways of thinking and behaving?
- How can discourse be analysed and researched?

Discourse: The Basics includes subject summaries, a glossary of key terms and suggestions for further reading. It will be of particular relevance to students of language and the social sciences but also useful to all students who are interested in how meanings are made.

Angela Goddard is a Professor of English Language, a UK Higher Education Academy National Teaching Fellow and Chair of Examiners for English Language A Level at a UK examination board.

Neil Carey is Principal Lecturer for Internationalisation in the Faculty of Health, Psychology and Social Care at Manchester Metropolitan University, UK.

THE BASICS

For a full list of titles in this series, please visit www.routledge.com/The-Basics/book-series/B.

DISCOURSE

THE BASICS

Angela Goddard and Neil Carey

Routledge
Taylor & Francis Group

LONDON AND NEW YORK

First published 2017
by Routledge
2 Park Square, Milton Park, Abingdon, Oxon OX14 4RN

and by Routledge
711 Third Avenue, New York, NY 10017

Routledge is an imprint of the Taylor & Francis Group, an informa business

© 2017 Angela Goddard and Neil Carey

British Library Cataloguing-in-Publication Data
A catalogue record for this book is available from the British Library

Library of Congress Cataloging-in-Publication Data
Names: Goddard, Angela, 1954-author. | Carey, Neil (Psychologist)
Title: Discourse : the basics / Angela Goddard and Neil Carey.
Description: Milton Park, Abingdon, Oxon : Routledge, [2017] |
    Includes bibliographical references and index.
Identifiers: LCCN 2016052591| ISBN 9780415856539 (hardback) |
    ISBN 9780415856553 (pbk.) | ISBN 9781315193311 (ebook)
Subjects: LCSH: Discourse analysis—Study and teaching. | Discourse
    analysis—Textbooks.
Classification: LCC P302 .G59 2017 | DDC 401/.41—dc23LC record
    available at https://lccn.loc.gov/2016052591

ISBN: 978-0-415-85653-9 (hbk)
ISBN: 978-0-415-85655-3 (pbk)
ISBN: 978-1-315-19331-1 (ebk)

Typeset in Bembo
by Swales & Willis Ltd, Exeter, Devon, UK

For Adrian and Murry

CONTENTS

FOREWORD

Every academic subject area uses its own discourse – a language that expresses that subject's particular perceptions of the world. As well as using academic discourses, some subjects go one step further and analyse them.

This book is aimed at those interested in the topic of discourse, regardless of their academic backgrounds. Of course we believe that every academic subject should involve the analysis of discourse; and, for those who are new to the idea of discourse analysis, it is hoped that the book offers some clear explanations of why it is important. But we are also mindful of readers who come to this book from academic areas that have a history of discourse analysis. For those readers, we hope to offer some explanations of where different approaches have come from, and to highlight some key principles behind different traditions.

Our own starting points have included English Literature, English Language, Linguistics, Communication and the Social Sciences, as teachers and researchers in the UK and internationally. Our interest in writing this book has arisen from many years of observing the difficulties students have faced in trying to understand a term that appears to mean so many different things. We have seen for ourselves how academic subjects often have ingrained, taken-for-granted understandings of the concept of discourse, so much so that explanations are not deemed necessary – a classic example of the power of discourse to make ways of thinking seem 'only natural'.

As well as a confusion surrounding terms and approaches, we have also observed the ways in which academic territories constrain the exploration of discourse, leading to a partial focus. Students can sometimes produce a good analysis of the internal mechanisms of a text, of its 'textuality', but fail to see the larger social context that produced it and to which it contributes. On the other hand, students can offer a perceptive analysis of larger social phenomena but fail to link their ideas with textual evidence. We hope that this book amply illustrates the mutual benefits of both perspectives and helps to show why discourse can only be fully understood as an interdisciplinary subject.

DEFINING DISCOURSE

AIMS OF THIS CHAPTER

This chapter will:

- offer some definitions of discourse and text;
- explain why there are different definitions of these terms; and
- outline how the rest of the chapters will work.

WHAT DOES THE WORD 'DISCOURSE' MEAN?

This question cannot be answered fully without taking the content of the whole book into account. However, as a basic starting point it is possible to identify some of the varied ways in which the term 'discourse' has been, and continues to be, used. This is the main task of the sections that follow.

DISCOURSE AND ITS RELATIONSHIP WITH TEXT

The term 'discourse' comes from Latin 'discursus', meaning 'to run to and fro'. In all the varied uses of the term, both in everyday contexts and in more specialist academic fields, there is a commonly shared concept of discourses as expressions of ideas that are put out into the world and that 'run to and fro' in one form or other.

Sometimes the term 'discourse' can suggest a specific form – that of speech. In the field of **Linguistics**, 'discourse analysis' has historically focused on stretches of spoken language, while 'text' has tended to refer to written material. While this is no longer necessarily the case, you need to be aware that if you are looking at older books and articles within the language studies area, the focus of the writers might well be on these different **modes**.

In contemporary books about language use, you will see both 'text' and 'discourse' used to refer to both speech and writing or, indeed, to multimodal communication, where there are hybrid forms such as SMS or social media posts that share qualities of both modes. Although the two terms can therefore be used interchangeably to describe any mode of language use, they can express difference in terms of the scale of communication and the breadth of perspective involved, with 'text' suggesting more of a micro-focus and 'discourse' a wider scope. Carter and Goddard (2015: 2), who write from a language perspective, sum this up as follows:

> While a 'text' has been seen more as a single artefact, 'discourse' has tended to refer to more extensive communication – a cluster of repeated representations, or interactions of some length and substance. . . . The different orientations suggested by the terms can be exemplified with reference to SMS usage. We talk about 'text messages' (or 'txt messages', where people are at pains to distinguish SMS from other kinds of text), referring to the digital artefacts we compose on phone keyboards. But we can also talk about 'the discourse of SMS', in which case our focus moves away from individual compositions towards a larger-scale view of the nature of this form of communication. Such a shift moves us beyond the finer details of the language features towards a greater understanding of who might use the communication, and where, when and why they might do so, as well as the longer-term social implications of its use.

A DIFFERENT VIEW OF 'TEXT'

The explanation above is based on a linguistic perspective, assuming that a text contains some verbal language. However, for other disciplines – notably the **Social Sciences** – a text does not necessarily have to involve language at all, and could just as easily be a physical object or even an empty space.

Social Science disciplines see social life itself as having 'textuality'. Here, the idea of text is taken as an **analogy** by which phenomena in the social world might be interpreted. The textual nature of social life implies that our lives are lived through story and **narrative**. As such, we are a product of the stories that are told about us and the stories we tell for and about ourselves. Indeed, there is an increasing recognition – even if unevenly – across and within some Social Sciences that the academic knowledge created by its **disciplines** also adopts particular linguistic patterns, thus making the language of the academic subject itself of interest to discourse analysts.

The emphasis on the textual nature of life – whether academic or social – is one that can be applied to objects in the world. From this perspective, the idea of 'text' is extended and applied to 'reading' material objects in the social world. Material objects generate meaning because they are thoroughly enmeshed in the social fabric of our world. Marketing and branding activities by retailers ensure that **commodities** become associated with ideas beyond their core purpose: cars, cosmetics, technology, bags and many of the other objects that constitute our daily life signify meaning beyond their basic functionality. Through a complex interplay between the objects themselves, and our desire for and use of them, material objects acquire meaning beyond their intrinsic value. In the process of buying and using these commodities – referred to in general terms as **consumption** – the objects are imbued with and confer social values including status, prestige and power within the broader social order of capitalism. Simultaneously, **social identities** are fashioned through such practices of consumption as individuals make lifestyle choices from among the relatively limited range of products available in the marketplace.

Paul Baker (2008: 1) provides an example of one of the many choices we are faced with in everyday contexts. In this account, his 'text' is a muffin – the type of individual cake that is sold in many coffee outlets.

Recently, I stopped at a coffee shop on the way home to get a drink and a muffin. At the counter, I noticed that the range of muffins on display had been labelled according to their 'gender', with the larger ones tagged 'male' and the smaller ones, 'female'. Normally, I would have chosen a small muffin as I wasn't very hungry. But I paused. I suddenly felt a bit 'girly' buying a small muffin, and, as a gay man, I didn't want to feel as if I was conforming to a stereotype of gay men as being like women or effeminate. So buying the large 'man'-sized muffin felt more appropriate. But I didn't really want a large muffin, and I didn't want to feel as if I was conforming to the expectation that men should eat larger muffins, or that I was somehow 'denying' my sexuality. Whatever choice I made, it seemed that I would be confirming someone else's expectations, that my behaviour could be predicted and explained – 'he bought the small muffin because he's trying to show he doesn't agree with stereotypes even though he confirms the "gay" stereotype' or 'he bought the large muffin because he's a conformist with internalized homophobia'.

Baker's example here highlights how the most mundane objects carry social meaning beyond their obvious function. Although Baker's work is firmly located in a tradition of language analysis, his work is akin to that done by other social scientists, including sociologists and geographers who 'read' social objects, practices and spaces as texts. Adopting a **Cultural Studies** approach, Barker and Galasinski (2001: 5) suggest that 'text is any phenomenon that generates meaning through signifying practices. Hence, dress, television programmes, advertising images, sporting events, pop stars, etc. can all be read as texts'.

No aspect of the physical world is too mundane for consideration as a text. In fact, it is the very ordinary, seemingly trivial nature of everyday encounters – termed *banal* by Billig (1995) – that forms the basis of their power.

DISCOURSE AND COMMUNITIES OF PRACTICE

'Discourse' as used so far has described a scale of activity or a breadth of perspective. It can also refer to expressions of ideas that come from a very specific area of human activity. Discourse in this case refers to a linguistic **register** that has evolved through group usage, where members of a community share knowledge of how things are done (including how communication is done) as part of their group identity. This idea is the basis of the concept of a **discourse community**, or a **community of practice**, and examples are most easily illustrated from occupational contexts. An example is given below, from the air transport community. The extract is from an interaction between an airline pilot and two different air traffic controllers in Canadian airspace:

Key:

AC 452 = Air Canada 452 (the aircraft)

ATC = Air Traffic Control. (There are two of these below: one at the airport terminal and another called 'Toronto Center'.)

128.800 MHz Toronto Terminal – (Departure)
(13:25)

AC 452: "Departure, good afternoon it's Air Canada 452 with you out of 1 point 3 for 5 thousand"

ATC: "Air Canada 452 good afternoon, radar identified maintain 7 thousand"

AC 452: "Roger, maintain 7 thousand"

ATC: "Air Canada 452, after noise abatement turn heading 0–9–0"

AC 452: "Right heading 0–9–0 after noise, Air Canada 452"
(13:26)

ATC: "Air Canada 452 climb to flight level 2–3–0"

AC 452: "Climb to flight level 2–3–0, Air Canada 452"
(13:27)

ATC: "Air Canada 452 contact Toronto Center on 1–2–7–0"

AC 452: "Toronto Center on twenty seven zero Air Canada 452, good day"
124.675 MHz Toronto Center – (Picton Sector)
(13:33)

AC 452: "Center it's Air Canada 452 with you climbing through twenty two point five"

ATC: "Air Canada 452 identified, maintain 3–3–0"

AC 452: "Ah, we'd prefer 2–7–0 as a final for today"

(continued)

(continued)

ATC:	"Roger, climb to 2–7–0 for Air Canada 452"
AC 452:	"Thank you, Air Canada's 452"
	(13:35)
AC 452:	"Ah center, Air Canada 452 would like to try level 2–4–0"
ATC:	"Roger your request, maintain 2–4–0"
AC 452:	"Maintain 2–4–0, Air Canada 452"

Although the language shown in the example is a particular type of discourse, some of it is still understandable by ordinary members of the public. This is partly because some of the words and structures are the same as mainstream English; it is also because non-specialists have become familiar with this type of language from **media representations** in films and documentaries. We are aware from such representations, for example, that the language is part of a larger regulatory system where actions accompany the words: the speakers are performing actions as a result of, and alongside, their spoken negotiations. From a language studies perspective, this is sometimes referred to as 'language-in-action' to illustrate its heavily context-bound nature.

Clearly, we are not all part of every discourse community. Nevertheless, we may have an idea – accurate or otherwise – about the type of language used within that group. This means that different types of discourse can be referred to, with an assumption that there is some general knowledge of how language is used in that context. Two examples of such references are given below.

These examples were among fifty samples produced by a search for the term 'discourse' within the British National Corpus (BNC), a computer-based searchable archive of 100 million words:

At the level of *parliamentary discourse* the net effect was a gradual transformation of the field of the political.

(Italics added)

As a political strategy it was highly effective, successfully confronting the *medical discourse* which lay behind regulation.

(Italics added)

The examples, originally from a book called *Dangerous Sexualities* (Mort 2000), refer to the language habitually used within two further specialist groups – members of parliament and members of the medical profession respectively. The book would have focused on the language of these two groups because they were very influential in shaping public ideas about sexuality.

Corpus-based research, exemplified by the search for the word 'discourse' on the previous page, is a relatively recent research method used particularly within language studies but also increasingly across many other academic fields. The search was a very general one for a single term, and the BNC is a compilation of many different sources, specialist and non-specialist, spoken and written. However, there are also specialist corpora that draw their data from the language use of particular communities or contexts, and these can be searched for not just single items but repeated (or expected but absent) structures. Corpus research can sometimes confirm our intuitions about how language is used; it can also overturn our assumptions and reveal a very different story from that based on assumptions and media representations.

An example of the latter is given in work by Kim and Elder (2009) on the communication patterns between Korean airline staff – pilots and air traffic controllers – and their American equivalents. A view that is often aired in the **mass media** is that people who use English as a second or additional language (EAL) in professional contexts such as airline communication might cause difficulties and misunderstand instructions. There are even suggestions that this might be the source of accidents. Kim and Elder's research, based both on digital recordings and interviews with members of the respective airline communities, reveals that miscommunication was often the result of *native speakers* not using the agreed specialist words and phrases. Native speakers sometimes abbreviated or elaborated their language, and at other times used opaque idioms.

Another example of corpus research on a particular community can be seen in Michael Nelson's (2000) research at Manchester University on business English. He compared a corpus of English as used in business contexts with the more general BNC corpus in an attempt to identify whether there was such a thing as 'business **lexis**' (vocabulary).

Nelson found what he describes as 'a **semantic field** of business' involving a limited number of semantic categories: business people, companies, institutions, money, business events, places of business, time, modes of communication and lexis to do with technology. With reference to places, the following were in evidence in the business corpus:

premises, department, boardroom, depot, office, division, marketplace

but none of these occurred:

town, county, village, opera, prison, castle, library, palace.

Also used far less in the business corpus was lexis referring to negative states.

A very different research method was used by Swales (1998) to explore the discourse of different academic communities. Far from there being a single type of language that is 'academic', each subject field has its own specialist terms and particular ways of looking at the world. Swales used what he called a 'textographic' approach, combining the idea of the study of texts with the term **ethnography**, which refers to the study of a community from the perspective of an insider. He visited different academic departments within a university and analysed various aspects of their textual output, including departmental notice boards, and reported on the differences he found.

Definitions of what constitutes a discourse community, or community of practice, vary. Lave and Wenger (1991), who first developed the idea of a community of practice, referred to ideas of mutual engagement between members, regular interaction and a sense of joint enterprise involving a shared repertoire of language use and practices. In other words, it's about the way groups do things, the ways they interact, their beliefs and values, and the relationships between them. Since the original concept of a community of practice was articulated, the idea of 'community' has spread beyond face-to-face interaction as a result of the Internet, producing research on how groups who have never met evolve forms of online discourse that act as a badge of membership.

'LITTLE D' DISCOURSE AND 'BIG D' DISCOURSES

The idea of expressions of beliefs and values brings us to a third way that the term discourse can be used. The previous section included examples from the BNC that were quotations from a book called *Dangerous Sexualities*. In discussing these examples, the phrase 'public ideas about sexuality' was used. These ideas can themselves be seen as a discourse – or, rather, a number of inter-related discourses, discourses in the plural. This time we are not talking about a particular mode of communication, or any particular group in society. This is a broader idea of discourse, being spread across many instances and being harder to pin down to a single person or group, or type of communication. Gee (1990: 142) terms this 'Discourses with a capital D', to differentiate this perspective from a focus on individual instances of discourse, which he terms 'discourse with a little d'. He sees the broader concept as consisting of combinations of 'saying–writing–doing–being–valuing–believing':

> These combinations I will refer to as 'Discourses', with a capital 'D' ('discourse' with a little 'd', I will use for connected stretches of language that make sense, like conversations, stories, reports, arguments, essays; 'discourse' is part of 'Discourse' – 'Discourse' with a big 'D' is always more than just language). Discourses are ways of being in the world, or forms of life which integrate words, acts, values, beliefs, attitudes, social identities, as well as gestures, glances, body positions and clothes.
>
> (Ibid.)

'Discourses of sexuality' might involve several sub-fields (such as ideas about sexual activity, sexual orientation, sexual health, eroticism) and appear anywhere across a society where messages are produced and received – for example, novels, educational pamphlets about sex education, popular magazines, films, poems, advertising. Baker's earlier example of buying a muffin (see pp. 3–4) shows how the wider discourses of gender and sexuality are implicated in even this seemingly trivial activity.

As Gee suggests, this wider definition of discourse really refers to whole ways of talking, writing, thinking and behaving. It is strongly associated with the work of the French philosopher Michel Foucault, and has been very influential across many different academic disciplines but particularly across the Social Sciences.

DISCOURSE AS AN EVERYDAY TERM

The term 'discourse' also occurs outside of academic domains, so it is important to say something about that, too. It is important because academic terms are discourses in themselves and a word can mean something different inside and outside of academic contexts. Outside of academic use, the term 'discourse' tends to refer primarily to spoken language, and to have connotations of formality. Look at the different ways of describing speakers engaged in talk, below. Although you would find some of these terms listed in a thesaurus as supposed synonyms, their **connotations** are very different. To get a sense of this, think of a topic – for example, food or holidays – and imagine how that topic would be treated in each of the scenarios below. What would be the difference between chatting about the topic of holidays and discoursing about them?

> To chat about a topic
> To talk about a topic
> To speak about a topic
> To discuss a topic
> To debate a topic
> To discourse on a topic

The formal connotations of 'discourse' and its association with speech, when used outside of academic contexts, can be seen in operation on p. 11, in two further examples of the term from the BNC search. In both cases, the formality of the term allows the writer to describe a character as socially awkward. The first example is from Jane Austen's *Sense and Sensibility*. It expresses a character's social unease via her anxiety about conversation drying up on formal occasions. This character thinks that having a child present is a kind of insurance against embarrassing silences as a child can provide the adults with something to discuss – for example, how much the child has grown, how they are doing at school, who they resemble and so on:

> On every formal visit a child ought to be of the party, by way of provision for *discourse*.
>
> (Italics added)

In this second example, from the novel *My Idea of Fun*, Will Self uses 'discourse' instead of 'speak' to suggest that the character was rather full of himself. In this case, the idea of 'running to and fro' is less about dialogue with another person and more about a pompous parade of his own opinions:

> He went on to *discourse* at length on the nature of fat.
>
> (Italics added)

DISCOURSE AND ACADEMIC SUBJECTS

You will already have realised that the term 'discourse' and the concepts it describes are not the province of any one subject area alone. Although for obvious reasons there are strong connections with language-based work, the 'bigger picture' idea of discourses as ways of thinking and behaving, and as expressions of beliefs and values, comes more from the Social Sciences than from traditional Linguistics. In addition, nowadays more and more academic fields are approaching the study of discourse and applying its insights to their own particular domains. This produces a complex picture – hence the need for this book.

Complexity can be challenging but it can also offer rich rewards. The chapters that follow will show you a range of different perspectives, but the book is not organised along the lines of each chapter covering a different subject area. Rather, the chapters take some important overarching concepts, dimensions and questions that are essential for an understanding of discourse – for example, the importance of context; ideas about language and 'reality'; how far a focus on social aspects can be taken; what is meant by 'representation'; how **metaphor** operates; discourse as a persuasive activity; what is meant by interactivity; how narratives work; and how the concept of identity has been viewed over time. Because this book is about discourse, it also includes ideas about how the academic discourse of writing-about-discourse could be approached. As ideas are discussed, specific academic fields or sub-fields will be referred to where possible and relevant; and these references, along with any specialist terms that may be unfamiliar, will be highlighted in bold on their first occurrence and glossed at the back of the book.

For those readers who are concerned about subject boundaries, it is not the intention of this book to muddy academic waters – at least, any more than they are already muddied. However, one of the aims of this book is to show what can be gained from joining some dots across traditional subject boundaries. **Interdisciplinary** research is often richer than single perspectives exactly because – as discourse study itself teaches us – there is always more than one way of looking at things.

Students often say they are worried about overstepping the boundaries of their particular subject field, incurring the dreaded criticism of 'irr' ('irrelevant') in the margin of their essay. In reality, this criticism from tutors often results from the fact that the writer has not set out clear parameters in the first place, to keep themselves focused. If a student is able at the outset to say which approaches they are going to take and why, then drawing on a range of subject fields will be viewed as a strength rather than a weakness. It is the aim of this book to give those writing about discourse the confidence to say how they are approaching their task, and as a consequence, a profound sense of pleasure at being able to lay bare some of the powerlines that lie behind our social lives.

2

DISCOURSE AND CONTEXT

A PRACTICAL EXERCISE

AIMS OF THIS CHAPTER

This chapter will:

- offer a practical starting point for analysing discourse;
- show the importance of context in any discourse analysis; and
- illustrate some of the different emphases that particular subject areas may have.

DISCOURSE AND CONTEXT

As will have become clear in Chapter 1, discourse in academic fields is by no means confined to the idea of formal texts or contexts. The term and the concept it describes is extremely wide ranging and can appear in many different guises, from the most formal speech by a head of state to the most informal note between people who know each other well. To add to this complexity, a single text could be defined and viewed in a number of different ways, depending on the particular academic 'lens' that is being used.

In the face of such broad scope it is important to have an accessible starting point. This will be provided below in the form of a practical exercise. This should show that although the idea of discourse may seem abstract and elusive, there are some tangible and predictable ways in which ideas about discourse can be applied.

A starting point for thinking about any text is the fact that every text arises from a context. Texts are produced by people at specific times and in specific places, with particular intentions, so the context of a text's production is a key factor in how it might be viewed, understood and judged. It might help in remembering the importance of context to think about the **morphology** of the word as con + text, where 'con' is a Latin prefix meaning 'with' or 'together'. You can see this prefix in many other ordinary words, such as connect, convene, confluence, consensus, congregate. As Spanish is based on Latin too, you can see the same element in chili con carne, 'chilli with meat'.

The context of the text in Figure 2.1 is that of a well-known chain hotel in the UK. As you can see from its outline, it was designed to hang from something, and in this case it was hanging from a bathroom towel rail. The original notice had black lettering on white plastic.

Having read the notice, put yourself in the position of the person standing in the bathroom and seeing this notice. How would you answer the questions below? The questions are based on the kinds of momentary, fleeting thoughts that any individual (i.e. not specifically a discourse analyst) might have when encountering an everyday text such as this. If you are in a group situation, use the opportunity to discuss these questions with others:

- Who is communicating with you? Why have they chosen this particular format and placement?
- How would you describe the type of language they are using?
- What type of person is being addressed? Do you feel that it's you? What assumptions are being made about you? How does the text make you feel?
- What does the text want you to do? What is it for?
- Does this text remind you of other texts you have seen? If so, which?

MACDONALD
HOTELS & RESORTS

Your bath fills
very quickly!
Even nipping out
to make a quick
phone call can
result in a flood,
so please take care

Figure 2.1 This bathroom notice exemplifies a hotel chain taking a novel
approach to communicating with its customers.

(Courtesy of Macdonald Hotels Group)

In fact, as this chapter proceeds, you will see that there is a great deal of commonality between these ordinary-looking speculations and the aspects that various academic fields have elaborated for detailed study and research.

In answering the questions on p. 14, you are carrying out a discourse analysis that pays particular attention to context. You are thinking about where the communication has come from, what it's like, why it's there, where it is situated, who it's aimed at and how it relates to other types of text. The explanations that follow describe some of these different aspects more fully.

WHO IS COMMUNICATING WITH YOU? WHY HAVE THEY CHOSEN THIS PARTICULAR FORMAT AND PLACEMENT?

The notice is, of course, part of a mass communication to all residents staying in the hotels run by the organisation, so from that perspective, it is a piece of **organisational discourse** (Grant et al. 2004). It may not be what immediately comes to mind when someone talks about 'the discourse of organisations' as we tend to think of this as being all about business memos and staff meetings. But the latter are examples of communication inside the organisation. There are also many examples of communication between organisations and their clients or customers, as here. And this relationship has to be very carefully calibrated because any message from a corporate enterprise communicates something about its identity, acting as a kind of branding.

There are many ways that the message contained in the notice could have been constructed in terms of its format – for example, it could have been stuck on the wall of the bathroom, as a permanent fixture. So why write the message on a piece of plastic and hang it by a hook from the towel rail?

The nature of its appearance can be linked with the relationship between the organisation that produced it and its intended audience. The hotel is part of a commercial world based on monetary exchange and where the power of the provider to tell the guest how to behave is constrained by the fact that the guest is paying for the privilege of bathing. So a notice casually hooked over a rail is more consistent with this idea of polite advice than a permanent, glued-on plaque might be, where the message might be read as more hectoring and imperative, as well as more impersonal and 'corporate'.

A focus on the nature of signs is the particular concern of the field of **Semiotics**, where the location and appearance of a piece of communication are seen as an integral part of its meaning. Semiotics is a large analytical field in its own right, and owes its development to a number of different figures, including a Swiss linguist, Ferdinand de Saussure (1857–1913), and an American philosopher, Charles Peirce (1839–1914). Saussure used the term 'semiology' to name a new area of study which he termed 'a science of signs', suggesting that the study of language as a system should take its place alongside all the other systems of meaning-making that human beings engage in. Although a semiotic analysis would have useful things to say about a sign in the literal sense, as here, the concept of a **sign** goes much wider and deeper than a simple notice. There is more about Semiotics in Chapter 4.

HOW WOULD YOU DESCRIBE THE TYPE OF LANGUAGE THEY ARE USING?

A discourse analyst doesn't have to be a language expert, but an analysis that doesn't include a consideration of any language that is present in a piece of communication is likely to be overlooking some potential meanings. We've already said that the notice originates with the hotel organisation, but it doesn't really sound like a corporate voice, does it?

The idea of a constructed voice that differs from that of the real author has a long history within **Literary Criticism** and the related field of **Narratology**, or studies of narrative. This is easy to exemplify in a very practical way if you think about the way novels have **narrators**, or figures who appear to be 'talking' to you, and how they are different from the real authors of the text. This idea of a constructed 'teller' of a story is one of the key distinctions between fiction and many non-fiction texts, where in the latter the narrator and writer are theoretically one and the same (although there are many examples of 'ghostwriters'). Compare, for example, a piece of detective fiction with a piece of 'true crime' journalism or an autobiography.

Although the hotel notice was clearly constructed by a real person, he or she would have been someone in the hotel's communication department; or perhaps the notice was produced by an advertising copywriter. Either way, in a discourse analysis of this type, the real person is irrelevant: the focus needs to be on the kind of person who *appears* to be communicating – in other words, the constructed persona of the narrator.

The language of the narrator seems quite informal, as if this is someone leaving a personal note as a helpful reminder. The exclamation mark suggests a personal touch, and the phrase 'nipping out' suggests informality – something you might hear more frequently in casual speech between friends than in formal writing aimed at strangers. This phrase could also suggest a level of growing regionality within **international English**, in the sense that UK-based English may become divorced from internationally used varieties. In a search of the Global Web-based English (GloWbE) corpus, which is a corpus of global web-based English use, the phrase 'nipping out' – or other variants such as 'nipping round', 'nipping in', 'nipping in and out' – was exclusive to UK English, with no occurrences in the USA. (Other uses of 'nipping' on its own were also present in both sets of results, for example with reference to animal bites.)

If you want to think in more detail about the level of formality in the bathroom notice, look at the two further versions of the notice on p. 19. How would you describe the language in each example, and how does changing the language change your idea of who is addressing you? To go further, try writing your own versions of a notice, using different levels of formality. (A thesaurus is a useful source of synonyms.) Creative re-writing exercises are a good way to support critical skills and constitute a well-known literary-critical method for critiquing literary texts: see Pope (1994), who terms this approach **textual intervention**.

Here are two re-creations of the bathroom notice. What differences are there between these and the original version?

Etiquette en toilette

When partaking of your ablutions, be advised that the water in the bath accumulates rapidly, and that absenting yourself from your quarters in order to engage in telephone communication may be a hazardous enterprise and could cause a deluge, therefore please exercise caution.

Don't cause a flood

The bath fills up in a flash. Your phone call can wait.
Don't be a careless idiot. Pay proper attention to what you are doing.

The next question on the list of bullet points set out earlier is as follows:

WHAT TYPE OF PERSON IS BEING ADDRESSED?

If you look at the two versions of the notice above (and any further versions you've written), you'll be aware that the language choices create an identity for the narrator, constructing a sense of a particular type of person 'speaking'. Language use always involves choices, and those choices always have implications. For example, the first 'speaker' above uses some very formal Latin- and French-based **polysyllabic** vocabulary, suggesting an educated speaker being excessively polite, to the point of comical exaggeration. The vocabulary items chosen – 'ablutions' instead of 'washing', 'deluge' instead of 'flood' – show that a range of options exist in the English language (or indeed any language), and this range is termed a **paradigm** within Semiotics. Paradigmatic relationships are based on the idea that one item could be substituted for another.

The language items selected are also in a **syntagmatic** relationship, combining with others. For example, in the same text, the **euphemistic** choice of 'ablutions' instead of 'washing' combines within one long complex sentence with the **modal verbs** 'may' and 'could', suggesting hesitancy and a delicate reticence. In contrast, the second version uses ordinary, largely monosyllabic words which produce an informal register, to the point of slang. However, this informality doesn't produce a sense of friendliness: quite the opposite. The short sentences are fired off one after another and sound hectoring as a result of the use of **imperatives** which issue commands to behave in a certain way.

It follows that the language of the various narrators has a strong effect on how, as a reader, you feel you are being defined and positioned by the communicator, and how you understand the intention behind the message. For example, you might decide that the first fictional text is a joke, given how out of place such formal language would seem for such a potentially simple piece of information-giving in a hotel bathroom. But, humorous or not, it is very indirect in the way it addresses a notional reader. This figure – the person who appears to be being addressed by the narrator – is termed the **narratee**. Like the narrator, the narratee is a fictional figure, this time on the receiving end of the communication. In contrast to the indirectness of the first fictional text, where the narrator hardly dare mention that the narratee might be careless enough to cause a mishap, the second text positions the narratee as a figure that is highly likely to be witless enough to cause a disaster, so has to be controlled and managed by a series of curt 'do's and don'ts'.

The original notice, like the two fictional ones, has direct address – 'your bath' – and there are obviously real, flesh-and-blood residents who will read the message. But the type of 'you' that 'you' are in textual terms is, as suggested earlier, heavily dependent on the language choices that have been made by the writer. Going a little deeper into the structure of the original text reveals that responsibility for any likely flood is expressed very indirectly, even though the register used is fairly informal. In the sentence structure, the subject (i.e. the element responsible for the action of the verb) is not 'you' – it is 'nipping out' that might result in such an event. A focus in detail on how linguistic items are arranged as part of considering issues of power, blame and responsibility is the particular concern of the field of **Critical Discourse Analysis**, but this is not the only field to give prominence to language use. For example, **Stylistics** and studies of

Rhetoric also focus on how language is organised and patterned. Linguistics covers many varied aspects of language use, including ideas about formality, some of the differences between spoken and written discourse, and regional variations in language. The latter is the particular focus of Sociolinguistics, where the emphasis is on language and social groups.

WHAT DOES THE TEXT WANT YOU TO DO?

This question is clearly connected with the previous one in that the text constructs a narratee who is the kind of person desired. However, real readers are not robots. Texts have purposes in the world, but that doesn't mean that we have to go along with the ideas in them. Texts can be resisted, and readers can choose to position themselves in ways where they do not conform to the idealised figures they are supposed to identify with.

The idea of purpose is at the basis of the classifications referred to as **genres**. There is no easy definition of this concept – which means 'type' – because different subject areas have different interpretations of it. In Literature, the term tends to refer to the three main literary genres of prose, poetry and drama; in Linguistics, genre can be any type of text, literary or otherwise, and can include speech as well as writing, and multimodal discourse as well. In **Media Studies**, the term is as likely to be referring to film as it is to any written text. Genres can be defined by many parameters, including their language features, their content and their social functions or purposes. Even thinking about the latter is not straightforward, for it is rare for a text to have a single purpose. For example, even though the overt purpose of the bathroom notice is to prevent negligent accidents, it also serves covertly to articulate the company's profile, or 'branding'. It is not a piece of communication from an individual, even though the narrator might appear to have a persona; the insignia and the company name remind us that behind this fictional figure there is a large corporation at work.

What genres are for, how to define them, how they change, how they are learned and how they relate to the power structures in any given society are all big questions that cannot be answered simply. There are so many issues to explore that there is a distinctive field of **Genre Studies** where **Genre Theory** is applied to specific examples.

DOES THIS TEXT REMIND YOU OF OTHER TEXTS YOU HAVE SEEN?

Fundamental to the idea of genre is the perception that texts do not exist in isolation, but form networks of relationships with other texts. As with the term genre, the associated term **intertextuality** can be found in more than one subject area. It is, however, particularly associated with the work of two literary critics and philosophers, Mikhail Bakhtin (1895–1975) and Julia Kristeva (1941–). Intertextuality refers to the way in which one text can refer to or echo another, with the idea that the meaning of any one text is partly derived from its relationship with others; and that it is partly through our repeated acquaintance with textual patterns that we are able to recognise individual texts as belonging to wider discourses.

So, for example, you perhaps recognised the bathroom notice because you have seen other advisory texts like it, in the same kind of setting – instructing you how to use the shower, or warning you not to slip, or reminding you to keep the shower curtain inside the bath, or suggesting how you can preserve the planet by re-using your towels. Or you might have classified the bathroom text as part of 'hotel discourse', seeing it not so much as something to do with a bathroom as such but more to do with the very many notices that corporate settings generate as part of managing the behaviour of large numbers of people. Or you might have seen the text as an example of a discourse of tourism and **geo-politics**, indicative of a world where certain groups of people get to travel and stay in hotels, take luxurious deep baths and make important phone calls – in which case, the text would be unrecognisable to people outside of that world. But to those people who do recognise it as part of a discourse, it acts as a touchstone of reality – 'I recognise this discourse, therefore I am in this kind of world'.

The next two chapters explore more fully the idea of discourse and 'reality' from different perspectives. Chapter 3 draws on Linguistics for ideas about language and thought, while Chapter 4 uses concepts from Semiotics and **Sociology** to explore wider issues of discourse, culture and communication.

3

LANGUAGE, THOUGHT AND DISCOURSE

AIMS OF THIS CHAPTER

This chapter will:

- critique the idea that language is a transparent medium;
- help you to see the role of language in constructing a sense of 'reality'; and
- start to explore connections between language, thought and discourse.

'A WORLD THAT IS SILENTLY TAKEN FOR GRANTED'

The sociologists Berger and Luckmann, in their pioneering study of the sociology of knowledge, *The Social Construction of Reality* (1991), saw language as one of the means by which people constructed a sense of reality. Language, they claimed, 'objectifies' the world: its naming function produces a sense of the tangibility of objects, people and ideas, and frequently repeated interactions build up a picture of 'how things are'. Ideas about 'the nature of things' are never spelt out; instead, meanings are created via shared and unspoken assumptions that are embedded in language use.

Berger and Luckmann saw the power of language as residing in its very unexamined ordinariness:

> It is important to stress that the greater part of reality-maintenance is implicit, not explicit. Most conversation does not in so many words define the nature of the world. Rather, it takes place against the background of a world that is silently taken for granted.
>
> (Berger and Luckmann 1991: 172–3)

Any work of discourse analysis therefore needs to start from an examination of what is 'silently taken for granted' in language use. What follows is some coverage of historical assertions about language and thought, and an explanation of why the questions that have been raised in this area are important for understanding discourse.

HOW FAR DOES LANGUAGE DEFINE OUR REALITY?

> Die Grenzen meiner Sprache bedeuten die Grenzen meiner Welt. (The limits of my language mean the limits of my world.)
>
> (Ludwig Wittgenstein, from the *Tractatus Logico-Philosophicus* (1922))

This famous statement from the German philosopher Ludwig Wittgenstein is part of a long history of thought and speculation about the relationship between language and the world around us. His view was that language sets up its own boundaries within which we perceive the world – in other words, we don't just see what is naturally around us; instead, we see what our language makes us see.

Much the same idea was put forward in a more elaborated way by the early linguist-**anthropologists** Edward Sapir (1885–1939) and Benjamin Lee Whorf (1897–1941) who studied First Nation (Native American) languages. Their concept was that learning and using a particular language was rather like donning a pair of spectacles that forced the wearer to look in a specific way. This was because, in their view, language is not a neutral, transparent system of labelling; instead, it is a fundamental part of the way patterns of thinking are established. This idea came to be known as the **Sapir–Whorf Hypothesis** and its essence can be seen in this statement by Whorf (1940: 229):

> We dissect nature along lines laid down by our native language. The categories and types that we isolate from the world of phenomena we do not find there because they stare every observer in the face; on the contrary, the world is presented in a kaleidoscope flux of impressions which has to be organized by our minds – and this means largely by the linguistic systems of our minds. We cut nature up, organize it into concepts, and ascribe significances as we do, largely because we are parties to an agreement to organize it in this way – an agreement that holds throughout our speech community and is codified in the patterns of our language. The agreement is of course, an implicit and unstated one, but its terms are absolutely obligatory; we cannot talk at all except by subscribing to the organization and classification of data that the agreement decrees. We are thus introduced to a new principle of relativity, which holds that all observers are not led by the same physical evidence to the same picture of the universe, unless their linguistic backgrounds are similar, or can in some way be calibrated.

LINGUISTIC DETERMINISM AND RELATIVISM

Contemporary views differ on the degree to which language systems control our perceptions, thinking and behaviour. While few academics within language study fields would argue that there is no relationship between language and thought, the extent to which we are 'imprisoned' by language is still frequently debated. Clearly, we cannot be completely imprisoned, otherwise we would never see the need for language to change. The fact that we can see a gap in the language available to us to describe our experiences and the things around us means that we must be able to think beyond our existing categories and labels. This is evidenced when there is pressure for language reform, from groups who claim that they are not represented fairly by existing names and descriptions. A negative take on this same process is called 'political correctness'.

The very fact that we have two contrasting labels for the same process, one positive (language reform) and one negative (political correctness), illustrates both the Sapir–Whorf Hypothesis in action and its limitations. It illustrates it through showing how a language choice can determine an attitude, or vice versa: using 'language reform' or 'political correctness' casts the process in a very different light, in each case. But it also illustrates the limitations of the hypothesis, because in the very act of having alternatives, we can escape from our language prison. It follows then that rather than a fully **deterministic** view of the relationship between language and thought, a more likely and workable explanation would be a **relativist** view: language does not completely determine thought, but it influences it in significant ways.

LANGUAGE AND REPRESENTATION

Although the Sapir–Whorf Hypothesis in its most extreme form has few adherents nowadays, the relativist version is still part of contemporary debates about language and **representation** – the role of language in constructing ideas about the nature of things and, more particularly, the nature of different social groups. The issue of representation links the topic of language and thought directly with that of discourse because if language influences our thinking, even to a small degree, then the language that we acquire and use to represent the world around us makes us think in certain ways. In turn, then, the discourses we produce as a result of thinking in certain ways help to construct a world that is unquestioned – 'silently taken for granted'.

Chapter 2 referred to the field of Semiotics. A key concept from that field, in its approach to language and representation, is that language is **arbitrary**. That means there is no logical relationship between a language item and the thing or idea it represents, beyond what has been established via social convention. This doesn't mean that language is meaningless. Quite the opposite: it means that language is richly influenced by culture, being constantly **mediated** by all the social factors that come into play whenever it is used.

Chapter 2 also referred to the idea of the 'sign'. Although this can refer to signs in the graphic sense, a 'sign' can also be an example of language use, something that 'signifies' or has meaning. However, meanings are not fixed. A sign is made up of a **signifier**, which in the case of language would be a linguistic item such as a word or a sound, and something **signified**, which would be the thing or person or idea referred to. The meaning of the sign is the whole of these aspects, including all the spaces between the signifier and the signified where individual experiences, group values and cultural norms help to shape the process of definition and interpretation.

As an example of what is meant by the 'spaces' in the previous sentence, take a single word, such as 'heart'. The word itself is a signifier, so what is signified, or being referred to, when this word is used? One answer could be that the word labels a muscular organ that pumps the blood through the body's circulatory system. But is that the end of the story? What about the idea of heart as the centre or core of something, as in 'the heart of the city' or 'artichoke hearts'? Or the idea of having the heart to do something; that is, having courage or bravery. Or being good-hearted or hard-hearted, referring to aspects of character? What about hearts as playing cards, or heart used as a verb meaning to like or love, as in the film title *I Heart Huckabees*? Context is obviously important: if we see the word 'heart' in a medical textbook we are more likely to think of the physical organ; and, going beyond verbal language for a moment, any graphic representation of the organ in a medical book will be a world away from the way it looks on a Valentine's card (hopefully). But many of the other language-based connotations of 'heart' above are heavily reliant on symbolic connections – the heart as a centrepiece, the heart as the basis of emotion and so on. These ideas are culturally produced and may well not translate across the boundaries of different languages and communities.

The arbitrariness of language makes it the servant of those who are able to assert and maintain power in any society, because they are then able to embed their own meanings in the discourses that constantly circulate. And it is only at points of challenge to those meanings that language stops being 'silently taken for granted' and becomes questioned.

The 1960s saw just such a challenge. Pressure for greater equality from social movements such as **feminism** brought language centre-stage because it was seen as a key aspect of how minority power groups were sidelined and kept subservient. For example, Robin Lakoff's *Language and Woman's Place*, published in 1975, claimed that women were **socialised** to 'talk like ladies', which meant being polite, unassertive and euphemistic in their expression. In turn, their language allowed them to be seen as less powerful. If women changed the nature of their language they were then in danger of being written off in another way – as being 'unfeminine'.

While Lakoff's focus was particularly on spoken interactions, other early feminist authors homed in on lexical and grammatical aspects in an attempt to reveal currents of thinking that were running through discourse. For example, Dale Spender's *Man Made Language* (1980) claimed that it wasn't sufficient to see language as simply a human construct: it was necessary to see it as encoding the experiences of those who had the power to define meanings in the first place – in this case, men. Spender's focus was particularly on the lexicon of English, and how lexical items not only brought a sense of validating reality to an experience, but brought a perspective as well. For example, she referred to the many terms for sexual behaviour and claimed that while men who had a healthy sexual appetite could be described as 'virile', there was no equivalent term for a female, who could only be one of two extremes – 'frigid' or a 'nymphomaniac'. She also noted that a range of terms for sexual intercourse – from the more polite term 'penetration' to the cruder term 'poking' – implied a male, active perspective and a passive female role. Spender claimed that if the female perspective had been **encoded**, we would have had a verb with the meaning of 'to enclose' rather than 'to penetrate', as the latter means 'to enter into'.

These examples are from a book written over thirty years ago, but the issue of language and representation, and of depictions of male and female figures, remains a contemporary concern and active field of language study. For example, Carter and Goddard (2015: 130, 174) refer to the way certain verbs work to build up representations of male and female behaviour in romantic fiction narratives. They note that male figures are often in active roles with **transitive verbs** of action like 'take' and 'kiss', in sentences such as 'he took her out onto the balcony and kissed her', while female figures are frequently associated with **intransitive verbs** of feeling such as 'she trembled', 'she sighed'. Try turning these expressions around and see how the depiction changes: 'she took him out onto the balcony and kissed him'; 'he trembled'; 'he sighed'. The seeming naturalness of the first version, and the oddness of the second version, illustrates the power of language not only to construct different perspectives, but to establish ideas about which perspective is the 'normal' one. This kind of detailed focus on language structures with the aim of revealing how positions of power are established and maintained in texts is the particular project of Critical Discourse Analysis, but there are many other discourse-analytic fields that will pay attention to language and meaning in this way – for example, approaches that have literary-critical origins such as Stylistics.

'A PROBLEM THAT HAS NO NAME'

The examples given centre on gender, but of course the possible role of language in helping to construct 'reality' has a much broader scope than this. The women's rights activist Betty Friedan (1921–2006) in *The Feminine Mystique* (first published in 1963) talked of 'a problem that has no name' to describe the way in which women in 1950s America felt unfulfilled and unhappy, despite having material comforts, because they did not have equal rights with men. Her phrase still resonates today because of a recurring question about the role of language: does having a name for something make it 'real'? Therefore, if we lack words to describe an experience, does that experience seem less believable? It does seem to be the case that the coinage of the terms 'sexism' and 'racism' in the 1960s to describe forms of discrimination on the basis of a person's gender or race made it easier to identify and classify (and ultimately make illegal) certain actions and patterns of behaviour. But, as Cameron (1995) points out, changing language alone will not change society; language change has to be part of structural changes in how people participate in society and live their lives.

'I LIVE IN A WORLD OF OTHERS' WORDS'

Given that language is a human construct, then it follows that the language we inherit is inevitably the result of those that have preceded us. The literary critic Mikhail Bakhtin (1895–1975), who is associated with the Russian **Formalist** school of criticism, saw all language as 'discursive' and 'dialogic', by which he meant that every use of language is shaped by the previous history of its use and is therefore part of a chain of communication through time. His quotation in the heading is an expression of that idea – that language is suffused with the cultural traces of 'others', so that creating meaning is not a simple case of starting with a blank canvas and inscribing it with our own definitions and connotations. It is more a case of re-fashioning what is already there:

> Language is not a neutral medium that passes freely and easily into the private property of the speaker's intentions; it is populated – overpopulated – with the intentions of others. . . . The word in language is half someone else's. It becomes one's 'own' only when the speaker populates it with his own intentions, his own accent, when he appropriates the word, adapting it to his own semantic and expressive intention. Prior to this moment of appropriation, the word does not exist in a neutral and impersonal language . . . but rather it exists in other people's mouths, in other people's contexts, serving other people's intentions; it is from there that one must take the word, and make it one's own.
>
> (Bakhtin 1992: 294)

The English language is shot through with cultural histories, from the **etymologies** of the many thousands of words that have come from different languages into English to the hidden connotations of the terms that remain current but that speak of a former society and its values. For example, the very different connotations of the phrases 'to mother a child' and 'to father a child' suggest the historically very different roles that have been ascribed to men and women around reproduction and childcare.

Sometimes it takes an act of creative invention or rule-breaking to expose those hidden associations. An example of creative invention is the relatively recent coinage of 'childfree' as a term to counter 'childless' and to offer a different perspective on the idea of not having children. An example of creative rule-breaking is the banner in Figure 3.1, celebrating the 5–0 defeat of England by the West Indies cricket team in the 1984 Test series. In the use of the term 'black' to describe something very positive, the banner cleverly articulates the innate disparity in the English language between the connotations of the terms 'black' and 'white'.

Figure 3.1 This clever piece of language play takes an existing meaning of 'whitewash' as used in a sports context – a series victory where the losing opponent fails to score – and creates a new word to describe the triumph of a black team over their white opponents.

(© Getty/Mark Leech)

LOST IN TRANSLATION

No two languages are ever sufficiently similar to be considered as representing the same social reality. The worlds in which different societies live are distinct worlds, not merely the same world with different labels attached.

(Sapir 1929)

The whole question of translation between languages offers some potentially interesting evidence about the extent to which language constructs a worldview for the speaker. If this idea is true, even to a small degree, then it follows that a bilingual speaker inhabits different 'worlds' when they switch between languages. The field of **Translation Studies** includes a focus on the extent to which it is even possible really to translate from one language to another, or whether the activity is more about giving a version that makes sense in the target language, within its cultural frame.

One of the problems in researching this area is that it is one thing to be fluent in different languages and to show great expertise in moving between them, but it is another to be able to stand back from one's own behaviour and describe it. Someone who has been able to do that is Eva Hoffman, who emigrated as a child with her parents from Cracow, Poland to Canada in 1959. No one in the family spoke any English and Hoffman's writings vividly evoke the experience of trying to understand the nature of language. She comes to realise that language is not simply a matter of labels for things and people, but rather something that connects us emotionally with our experiences and with whole frameworks of thinking and behaviour that endow language with meaning. She also comes to realise that her native Polish and the English she has to acquire do not always fit neatly in the way each language categorises the world.

Hoffman became a writer and academic, and in this extract from her book, *Lost in Translation*, she talks about a word that has no single equivalent in English, the Polish word 'polot'. She remembers her early education, then gives examples of 'polot' in action. She links the term with the values that are held dear in Polish society:

Or perhaps I am picking up notions about flair, and panache, and sparks of inspiration – tonalities of character that are the true Polish values, and that are encouraged by my peers and my schoolteachers, not to speak of the Romantic poetry we read. There is a romantic undercurrent to much of the education I get. What counts in a written composition – whether it's about our last school excursion or a poem by Mickiewicz – is a certain extravagance of style and feeling. The best compliment that a school exercise can receive is that it has *polot* – a word that combines the meanings of dash, inspiration and flying. *Polot* is what everyone wants to have in personality as well. Being correct and dull is a horrid misfortune. 'The good', in our eyes, is not a moral entity at all but spontaneity, daring, a bit of recklessness. Marek, in my mind, has *polot*. So did those Polish cavalrymen, about whom we hear so often, who went out to meet German tanks when the Nazis invaded. Chopin's *A Major Polonaise* coming over the loudspeakers in the last heroic moments of the Warsaw uprising, as bullets and grenades ricocheted through the streets – that is a gesture that captures the essence of *polot*. And *polot*, of course, is absolutely necessary in music; without it – without the flair, and the melancholy, and the wildness that ignite the sounds with fire and tenderness, you can practice all you want, and you won't come anywhere near greatness.

(Hoffman 2008: 71. Reproduced with the kind permission of Eva Hoffman and the Rogers, Coleridge and White Literary Agency)

Although Hoffman's focus in the passage is on the meaning of a single word, that term, and all the ideas associated with it, play a part in constructing notions of the personal qualities to aspire to in Polish society. From a language perspective, webs of meaning are not simply about the availability of terms, but significantly also about how those terms connect with each other to categorise things, people and experiences.

A further example from later in the book illustrates this idea in more detail. Hoffman compares the way the Polish and English languages categorise the terms 'friend' and 'acquaintance', then goes on to describe how she tries to understand the phenomenon called 'dating' in the teenage culture of Vancouver. These terms clearly exist in a network of connections and are hedged around with expectations of particular kinds of behaviour. Hoffman sees the term 'friend' in English as a very general, multi-purpose term, whereas in Polish, the term has connotations of strong loyalty and attachment bordering on love. So, while the young Hoffman feels uncomfortable calling a female classmate a 'friend', she cannot really opt for 'acquaintance' as that sounds very stilted in English. When she tries to make sense of Canadian behavioural rules around dating – for example, the point at which one's 'date' is expected to meet one's parents – she concludes that her exploration of language reveals a whole world of unspoken practices that are taken for granted by the members of the community she is trying to fit into: in the words of Brown (2001), she discovers that '[e]very immigrant becomes a kind of amateur anthropologist'.

Hoffman's experiences, and her ability to articulate the issues involved in trying to move between cultures and languages, are clearly unusual. But you might be able to approach similar questions if you think about some of the problematic gaps that exist in the language(s) that you know, as a result of social changes. For example, what do you call the person with whom you have a romantic relationship but are not married to? Your girlfriend/boyfriend? Partner? Lover? Does the term you choose depend on your age? Does your sexual orientation make any difference? If you know another language, are there different options there?

Sometimes, similar ideas can be expressed in another language but may have to be described in some very longwinded ways. For example, Swedish has a large group of words that describe different kinds of partnerships in terms of how people live. The stem word 'bo' (pronounced 'boo'), meaning 'live' or 'dwell', can have many prefixes, some serious and some playful, as follows:

Sambo:	a shortened form of samman-boende, 'living together'. This describes people in a romantic relationship who live together but are not married. Swedish laws around 'sambo' are stronger than those for UK 'common law' partnerships.
Närbo:	a romantic partner who lives nearby.
Särbo:	a romantic partner who lives a long way away.
Delsbo *(deltid = part-time):*	a couple who sometimes cohabit.
Helgbo *(helg = weekend):*	a couple who live at each other's places on alternate weekends.
Mambo *(mamma + bo):*	someone who still lives with his or her parents.

There are also gendered words for 'friends who are not lovers': 'tjejkompis' is 'a female friend but not a girlfriend', and 'killkompis' is 'a male friend but not a boyfriend'.

GOT A WORD FOR IT?

The big question that follows any investigation of the way different languages describe the world is whether people behave differently as a result, and whether they literally see different things. Here are some more examples, from different languages, of terms for which there is supposedly no equivalent in English (de Boinod 2005). Terms such as these are useful to think about with reference to the opportunities or constraints experienced by speakers, depending on the language they have available to them. They are also useful in considering what they suggest about the values of the society concerned. For example, does having certain language choices give speakers access to whole areas of activity, of thinking and behaving, that can be elaborated across the culture and that have further consequences – even regulatory and legal ones? This 'big picture' aspect of discourse will be explored further in the next chapter.

PASCUENSE (EASTER ISLAND)

Tingo: to borrow objects one by one from a neighbour's house until there is nothing left.

JAPANESE

Age-otori: to look worse after a haircut.

Arigata-meiwaku: an act someone does for you that you didn't want to have them do and tried to avoid having them do. They went ahead anyway, determined to do you a favour, and then things went wrong and caused you a lot of trouble. In the end, social conventions required you to express gratitude.

SPANISH

Duende: a climactic show of spirit in a performance or work of art, which might be fulfilled in flamenco dancing, bull-fighting, etc.

GREEK

Meraki: doing something with soul, creativity or love – putting something of yourself into what you're doing.

MANDARIN CHINESE

Guanxi: in traditional Chinese society, you can build up guanxi by giving gifts to people, taking them to dinner or doing them a favour, but you can also use up your guanxi by asking for a favour to be repaid.

KOREAN

Nunchi: the subtle art of listening and gauging another's mood. In Western culture, nunchi could be described as the concept of emotional intelligence. Knowing what to say or do, or what not to say or do, in a given situation. A socially clumsy person can be described as 'nunchi eoptta', meaning 'lacking in nunchi'.

NORWEGIAN

Forelsket: the euphoria you experience when you are first falling in love.

FILIPINO

Gigil: the urge to pinch or squeeze something that is unbearably cute.

YAGHAN (TIERRA DEL FUEGO)

Mamihlapinatapai: a look between two people that suggests an unspoken, shared desire.

CZECH

Litost: a state of torment created by the sudden sight of one's own misery.

MEXICAN SPANISH

Pena ajena: the embarrassment you feel watching someone else's humiliation.

GERMAN

Schadenfreude: the pleasure derived from someone else's pain.

4

LANGUAGE, SOCIETY AND DISCOURSE

AIMS OF THIS CHAPTER

This chapter will:

- explore how Semiotics can be used as a framework for helping to identify wider discourses; and
- exemplify how familiar and everyday signs provide a point of analysis to explore wider discourses.

TAKING PART IN DISCOURSE

In Chapter 1 it was suggested that discourse involves a process of 'running to and fro'. This has an obvious meaning when we think about being in conversation with another person. However, we can also use this idea of 'to and fro' in thinking about how we actively engage with written and visual texts of all kinds. Here we are suggesting that we are 'in conversation' with texts when 'reading' or 'decoding' them to make sense of those texts. We are also suggesting that in making sense of such texts in the everyday, we are also actively engaged in constructing ideas about ourselves and the social world in which such sense-making occurs.

Semiotics, which conceives of texts as a system of signs, provides a useful starting point in understanding how language and other symbols used in communication work as part of wider cultural codes. It allows discourse analysts to highlight how the sign systems that make up texts mediate the social world and, therefore, how we make sense of that social world. Semiotics is a highly complex area of study that was originally most closely associated with Linguistics (see Chapter 2) but has been adapted and developed by a variety of other disciplines in the Humanities and Social Sciences. For example, Semiotics is applied in the analysis of other complex sign systems like photographs, films, fashion and architecture.

Daniel Chandler's (2007) book as part of this *Basics* series provides a very helpful overview of some of the complexities associated with the development and application of Semiotics across a range of academic disciplines and will allow you more fully to appreciate these complexities. The following section introduces some basic and commonly understood ideas from Semiotics and provides a starting point for how you can begin to apply Semiotics in the analysis of everyday sign systems.

SIGNS IN SIGNS

As outlined in Chapter 2, a fundamental building block of Semiotics is the idea that 'signs' involve a relationship between a signifier (a word, sound, image, object) and something signified (an object, person, concept, idea). It was also stressed that the relationship between the signified and signifier is arbitrary but is mediated by social and cultural values that shape how signs come to have meaning.

Taking a set of pervasive and seemingly banal examples of a sign system, we can examine more closely this idea that the meaning available through signs is shaped by cultural understandings. Although not completely universal, toileting facilities are a feature of public spaces in many cultures. These public facilities, provided for the general population in public spaces or in commercial venues accessed by the public, are distinguishable from similar facilities that are common in most domestic spaces. For our purposes here, the most obvious way in which public toilets are distinguishable is that they are most usually denoted by clear signage. Many of these signs are familiar to most people, especially in the developed world, and they call attention to what, at first glance, might be seen as simply functional spaces.

A simple internet search for images of 'toilet sign' or 'toilet signage' will result in a startling array of signs. A good example of this variety can be found at http://losu.org/world/the-many-different-types-of-toilet-signs. Whilst some of the variety represents an attempt to inflect humour into the signs, other variations reflect differences in the local language or particular forms of dress within a culture. However, the most common signs used for toilets in public spaces have become fairly universal and are similar to or variants of those in Figure 4.1:

Figure 4.1 A typical set of toilet door signs used in public facilities.

(You should note here that the use of 'sign' in 'toilet sign' in everyday language is related to but distinct from the specialised use of the word 'sign' in Semiotics.)

In Semiotic terms, the sign here consists of the signifier (the stylised figure of a woman and a man) and the signified is either the toilet apportioned to females and males or the female and male who use such facilities. The familiar graphics of stylised figures denoting public toilets here are considered **iconic** signs in that the signifier seems to resemble that which is signified. This mode of signification is often distinguished from linguistic signs (e.g. the written or spoken words 'female/male' or 'women/men') which are considered **symbolic**. The difference between iconic and symbolic signs hinges on the level of cultural convention necessary for the signifier to be accepted as carrying appropriate meaning. Within Semiotics, iconic signs are sometimes conceived of as being less arbitrary, or more 'obvious' in their ability to represent the signified on the basis of the signifier. Other examples of iconic signs might include paintings, photographs and films. However, further exploration below demonstrates that even with iconic signs there is a great deal of cultural understanding that mediates meaning between signifier and signified, and this mediation helps in understanding how discourses are produced and reinforced in everyday meaning-making.

From the internet search for 'toilet signs', one of the most obvious similarities across the signs is that public toilets are, commonly, signed separately for males and females. At the surface level, female and male toilets are 'signed' by different and slightly contrasting shapes. As 'readers' of these signs we make sense of these differences in shape as denoting distinctions in dress styles most traditionally associated with gender roles. Here women are denoted as wearing a dress and males as wearing trousers. In the first instance, these denotations are associated with traditionally Western ideals of gender-appropriate dress, failing to represent the kinds of attire that both men and women traditionally adopt in a diverse range of cultural contexts – including those in which trousers have never been part of traditional attire or where trousers were traditionally the attire of both men and women. This simple point of analysis might well be a starting point for highlighting the ways in which Westernised ideals are a feature of broader processes of **globalisation** and are consequently reflected in the global spread of Western-inflected discourses. Indeed, some argue that with increased globalisation we are witnessing a **homogenisation** of culture to the detriment of more specific local cultures.

Second, the denotations of gender-appropriate dress can be seen, especially in contemporary Western contexts, as failing to represent the changing nature of gender-appropriate dress codes whereby women are just as likely to wear trousers as men. Both these points might seem banal or obvious. However, they help to make the point that in adopting a discourse-analytic approach we must be alive to that which seems obvious or 'natural' in a given cultural context. This aspect of discourse analysis can be most difficult when critically examining sign systems in the culture to which we, ourselves, belong.

At another level, the signs for public toilets denoting female and male might also be said to carry a series of meanings that have deeper cultural significance. These deeper-level associations attaching to Semiotic signs are referred to as connotations. For example, as well as reassuring us about which door to enter when accessing public toilets, the signs (and the separate doors on which they are located) reinforce taken-for-granted cultural understandings about hygiene and sanitation practices and about privacy and bodies. Most obviously, the signs suggest that such practices should normally be conducted on a strictly sex-segregated basis. In turn, these norms reinforce cultural assumptions about the binary and differentiated nature of gender: that there are only two genders, and that the differences *between* men and women are much more important than the many ways in which men and women are similar to each other. This latter point tends to ignore the ways that men and women from particular classes, races or nations often experience these aspects of their lives in common. Concomitantly, the signs might also be said to reinforce a whole series of assumptions about masculinity and femininity. Gershenson and Penner (2009) argue that gender segregation in public toilets is enmeshed in a long history about sex-role differentiation; the idea that anatomical and biological differences between females and males determine and legitimate the distinction of abilities, and unequal access and rights accorded women and men in society.

DISRUPTING SIGNS

The cultural differences between men and women connoted by the stylised male and female toilet signs are denoted by differences in traditional, Western modes of dress. The female figure wears what looks like a dress – the ultimate signifier of femininity (it is apposite here to contrast the social acceptability of women wearing trousers against the social strictures applied to men wearing dresses). Femininity marks femaleness as the necessary but unequal partner of maleness, and the dress is the defining mark of both sex segregation and the inequalities between men and women.

A recent advertising campaign – 'It was never a dress' – from a software company in the US (see Figure 4.2) has targeted the representation of femininity in the toilet sign for females. The campaign focuses on reconfiguring the triangular shape most usually interpreted as a dress. The campaign offers an alternative 'reading' of the shape, insisting that the triangle is actually the outline of a cape – slung over

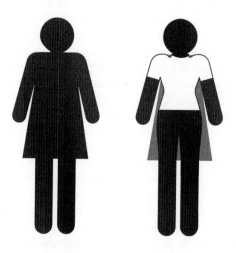

It was never a dress.

Figure 4.2 'It was never a dress' disrupts the traditional representation of femininity, making an alternative reading of the sign possible.

the shoulders and tied at the neck of the female figure – and is more akin to the kind of garment associated with superhero characters. The campaign's claim is that their reading of the female figure resists the traditional conception of femininity and replaces it with a more empowered conception of females and femininity.

The campaign's disruption of the familiar sign for female demonstrates a more general feature of Semiotic signs, explored by Stuart Hall in his analyses of how media (as complex signs) function in culture. Hall (1986) suggests that meaning is encoded in the production of sign systems that constitute communications. In this, Hall's argument is in line with many previous theorists who insist that the production of sign systems is governed by a set of conventions (according to genre, mode or medium), thus positioning signs as carriers of the meaning intended by their producers. However, Hall was also interested in how media were consumed by the public, and in debunking the idea that meaning was transmitted directly from media producer to consumer. Hall argued that, just as signs were encoded with meaning in their production, signs were also **decoded** for meaning by their readers, and there was not necessarily a one-to-one correspondence between the processes of encoding and decoding. In this argument Hall gives significant agency to the reader or consumer of signs. Hall identified three ideal types of 'reading position' that might be adopted in consuming texts. These positions, adapted from Chandler (2007: 194–5), are:

- Dominant reading: the reader fully shares the text's code and accepts and reproduces the preferred reading – in such a stance the code seems natural and transparent.
- Negotiated reading: the reader partly shares the text's code and broadly accepts the preferred reading, but sometimes resists and modifies it in a way which reflects their own position, experiences and interests.
- Oppositional reading: the reader, whose social situation places them in a directly oppositional relation to the dominant code, understands the preferred reading but does not share the text's code and rejects this reading, bringing to bear an alternative frame of reference (radical, feminist, etc.) in making sense of the text.

Further work by Hall emphasises how reading positions are changeable and dynamic and are dependent on the content and contexts in which texts are read. Despite these caveats, Hall's work underlines the idea that texts, and the signs that make them up, are unstable and open to negotiation on the part of both their producers and consumers. Having said that, questions remain about the ways in which reading positions, other than the dominant/preferred one, can actually have widespread effects and lead to changes in mainstream culture. In this respect, one might speculate where and how the 'It was never a dress' campaign outlined on pp. 42–3 will change mainstream ideas about femininity and femaleness.

REPRESENTATIONS AND REALITY

Language (whether spoken or written) and images are a system of symbols or signs which represent the world in which we live. In terms of discourse, representation 'refers to the use of language and images to create meaning about the world around us' (Sturken and Cartwright 2001). It seems like a very obvious idea that these symbols 'stand for' or represent the world as we understand it. However, this idea also implies that reality is always mediated by symbol systems and signs in the form of conversations, texts and images.

This central proposition further suggests that, in order to understand the world, we rely largely on those forms of representation that are culturally salient for us as members of that culture. This idea, that the real world is produced and interpreted in and through symbols, is known as **Social Constructionism**. In its most determinist form, this view of social life suggests that reality is always mediated through those symbols and signs for which we have agreed 'rules' of creation and interpretation. Language and other sign systems here are not seen as a neutral medium that merely transmits knowledge. Rather, language and images are also actively involved in constructing our sense of reality (see Chapter 3). According to this view, language is seen as constitutive: it constructs reality rather than merely just reflecting reality.

This conception of language and its relation to reality has important implications for thinking about and approaching the idea of discourse. It debunks the idea that anyone can 'tell it like it is' or 'keep it real' and recognises that any claim to 'keeping it real' is a particular form of argument that is deployed for particular purposes and in particular contexts. Similarly, it suggests that we are enmeshed in, and rely on, sign systems to understand our relation to the world around us – even when the rules and associations attaching to cultural signs are so familiar that they seem '**naturalised**'. This conception of language and its relation to reality has important implications for thinking about and analysing individual signs and the wider sign systems of which they are a part.

LOOKING BEYOND THE LABEL

An example of representation that may have immediate relevance to you is the sign 'student', a label that signifies certain kinds of roles and behaviour. However, these understandings vary across contexts and change over time. In terms of contexts, the behaviours and roles both expected of and adopted by learners will certainly depend on whether they attend a school, college or university. Indeed, there will be variation within each of these levels of education depending on a range of variables, including the availability of education and the resources invested in particular contexts. Equally, 'student' will signify differently depending on the dominant **pedagogical** culture that exists in the country or educational system in which learning takes place: some pedagogical cultures adopt a **didactic** mode whilst others adopt a more interactive and **dialogic** mode of learning.

Similarly, who is considered a student and what is signified thereby is different in contemporary society than it was a century ago. Indeed, such changes can occur over much shorter time spans. As an example, recent UK governments have replaced free, state-funded university education with a system by which the student is responsible for paying tuition fees directly to the university (usually via loan systems). This change in funding arrangement has had interesting repercussions for how university students are constructed and see themselves. Concomitantly, there has been a shift in contemporary discourses of higher education within the UK context. In the recent past, 'student' might primarily signify a learner who was an apprentice to their professors and who was responsible for ensuring the success of their own learning. More recently, 'student' is more likely to signify a learner who is a consumer of educational services and can, therefore, hold their professors to account if they are not satisfied with the service they receive.

These recent changes shift the meaning attaching to the signifier 'student', rendering the position available to those who occupy the role as radically different from more traditional views about the aims of higher education and how students were part of that larger system. Indeed, some argue that the recent changes in how higher education is funded in the UK are the result of dissatisfaction with the ways in which higher education institutions traditionally conceived of the role of students. Proponents for such changes argue that a radical shift was required in rethinking the role of universities in society and that such changes could be achieved – at least in part – by challenging traditional constructions of the student.

It is on the basis of such a constructivist philosophy that a discursive approach to researching the social world and our relationships in it takes a great deal of its legitimacy. To explore this approach further with reference to the cultural changes in education that have been described, see Furedi (2009), Molesworth et al. (2010) and Brown (2013).

HOW FAR CAN YOU GO?

How far can a discourse-analytic approach go when it comes to unpicking the cultural values that lie behind a 'sign'? The rest of this chapter will take you on a journey to attempt to answer that question. Get ready for a ride.

GENDER AND DISABILITY

Referring back to the toilet signs explored earlier, adopting a discursive approach in studying them as Semiotic signs marks the fact that we are interested in understanding how the toilet signs maintain and reinforce taken-for-granted ideas about gender and, more specifically, gender differentiation. In effect, not only do these signs reflect the material reality that public toilets are, most usually, segregated according to gender alone, they also reflect and maintain a central and seemingly naturalised set of understandings about the binary and differentiated nature of masculinity and femininity.

However, the strict segregation of public toilets by sex/ gender that is most common is in stark contrast with those facilities provided for by people with disabilities (when such facilities are provided). At least in many Western contexts, the most common sign used when indicating public toilets for people who are disabled is quite distinct: the signifier is a stylised person sitting on what looks like a wheelchair. As well as signifying a set of 'specialist' toileting facilities, the sign also signifies those people who use these facilities. Many activists who campaign for disability rights are troubled by this sign, not least because it comes to reinforce the idea that people with mobility impairments who use a wheelchair 'become' the wheelchair, to the detriment of their wider identity. The sign is also criticised because it reinforces narrow and very particular assumptions about the form and nature of disabilities, failing to represent the wider range of conditions and impairments that render people disabled in and by society (Shakespeare 2014; Shildrick 2004).

Tom Shakespeare (2014) outlines some of the many ways in which disability is, and has been, constructed over time. With a particular focus on the UK, he tracks some of the wider activist and intellectual movements agitating for social and economic rights for disabled people over the second half of the twentieth century. These movements spanned the radical changes by which disability was treated in developed countries over this period. Such changes include: attempts to relocate people with disabilities away from large residential institutions into community-based housing; activist and advocacy campaigns to shift from medical discourses as the dominant way in which to frame disability, towards discourses that emphasised the social, political and economic aspects of disability; attempts to differentiate the central concept of impairment from the associated but independent concept of disability, and attempts to establish the rights of people who are disabled within national and international legal frameworks (see also Barnes and Mercer 2010). In doing so, Shakespeare highlights some of the many and contradictory ways in which dominant cultural ideas of disability have emerged in most developed countries, and which continue to shape – rightly or wrongly – policy and practice in emerging and underdeveloped countries (Grech 2015).

In the context of our explorations about how signs for public toilets reinforce cultural ideas about gender differentiation, it is apposite to think about how and in what ways this latter sign (and the physical spaces it signifies) constructs ideas of disabled people. Given that these signs do not conform to the strict sex/gender segregation highlighted for mainstream toilets, what might be signified about those who are disabled? Are people who are disabled gender-neutral or gender-free? Perhaps issues of gender are considered irrelevant in the case of people who are disabled. If this is the case, and given that the strict sex/gender segregation of toileting practices occurs within cultural contexts where heterosexuality is the norm, then in what ways does this type of sign construct people with disabilities as being less sexual or even asexual? This latter question, focused particularly on sexuality, has been explored extensively by activist and academic literatures as a way of highlighting some of the ways in which disability is socially constructed in Western contexts (see Kulick and Rydström 2015; Shildrick 2012). This latter type of critical analysis demonstrates the relational nature of discourses: exploring discourses of sexuality provides insights into dominant ideas about the construction of people who are disabled, and vice versa.

SIGNS HAVE HISTORIES

The systems of symbols, the signs, by which we understand both the world and our roles within it have developed over time and are significant for a specific culture or sub-group within a society. Some ideas get **sedimented** over time and are seen as taken-for-granted truths within a culture. Through this process of cultural sedimentation a social group develops a shared understanding of these signs and the concepts, things, groups and phenomena that are signified. Members of the cultural system are aware of such meanings, even if they are not fully conscious of the conventions by which those meanings come about. Often signs are so familiar that they seem naturalised.

Like all Semiotic signs, toilet signs too encode the beliefs and values of those cultures within which they came about and continue to exist. Shared toileting facilities have been, or continue to be, a common feature of most societies. The development of widespread public toilets came about largely with increasing urbanisation and the desire to protect public health through improving urban sanitation and hygiene standards. Early public toilets were largely for the use of men and this reflected traditional ideas that privileged the public realm as masculine whilst femininity was largely associated with private and domestic spheres. However, urbanisation also meant that women were increasingly required to enter the public realm either to work or to partake in leisure activities. Gershenson and Penner (2009) argue that the development of sex-segregated public toilets was a largely Western invention in the latter part of the nineteenth century and encoded culturally dominant ideals about the separation of bodily functions by gender whilst facilitating – rather begrudgingly – women's access to the public realm for sustained periods of time. The strict segregation of public toilet facilities also underscores a constellation of predominant social concerns about **moral hygiene** that were contemporary with such developments.

In Britain, moral hygiene was concerned with a broad range of issues including concerns about urban crime, prostitution and the rise of venereal disease, and an explicit recognition of the need to encourage the growth of a strong and healthy population to service the requirements of an expanding empire and rapidly developing industrialisation. Many of these concerns centred, either explicitly or implicitly, on the regulation and control of sex and sexuality (Mort 2000). Such regulation was largely targeted at women whose passive sexuality needed protection, and at the lower classes who were considered as either childlike in their sexual rampancy or almost bestial in their sexual incontinence. Within the context of such social concerns, establishing sex-segregated toilets became part of what was considered common sense – especially given that such bodily functions seemed so inextricably linked with sex and sexuality. This brief overview gives a simplified version of some of the complex histories leading to the rise of sex-segregated toilets and indicates how personal toileting practices became a matter of public and social concern. It highlights the efforts and social pressures that contributed to what now may appear as naturalised and taken for granted in urban and particularly Westernised contexts.

This kind of historical analysis is important to explore and uncover when investigating how discourses operate through signs that are familiar and apparently culturally neutral. The benefit of making explicit such histories marks the fact that the persistence of sex-segregated toilets, and the naturalisation of gender differentiation that is closely associated with it in contemporary Western societies, seems wholly at odds within those very cultural contexts where gender equality is extolled as the ultimate mark of progress and civilisation.

SIGNS OF ALTERNATIVE REALITIES

The issue of gender segregation in public toilet use is certainly not only an historical one or one that applies to the rights of disabled people. The gender-segregated nature of public toilets also reinforces a set of beliefs about gender in that they signify that gender conforms to a strict binary logic: that being male and female are mutually exclusive categories. Contemporary debates – largely informed by the toileting needs and rights of **transgender** and **gender-variant** people – continue to raise questions about the

Figure 4.3 A sign that attempts to go beyond the rigid binary distinctions of male and female.

fixed nature of gender and sexuality more generally, and about how language and symbol systems inform and reinforce these traditional ideas. For example, transgender and gender-variant people have argued for gender-neutral toilet facilities where their status outside the accepted gender binary is recognised, and they can feel safe from the law, violence and the kinds of social opprobrium that are commonly associated with anyone transgressing the gender divide (Gershenson and Penner 2009). Like feminist campaigns in the 1960s and 1970s which centred on the use of 'Ms' as an alternative to either Miss and Mrs as a form of address for women (and as an equivalent of 'Mr', which does not refer to marital status), contemporary 'trans' campaigns insist on 'Mx' to signify a refusal of the strict gender binary of male/female. The form of Mx also has a toilet sign associated with it (see Figure 4.3).

The toilet sign shown in the figure has been suggested as an alternative to the more common male/female ones to signify a gender that goes beyond the male/female gender binary. This sign attempts to disrupt the commonly assumed either/or binary of male and female genders, and demonstrates how social groups campaigning for social justice and change appreciate the importance of working at the level of Semiotic signs in attempting to achieve rights and equality.

The campaign for gender-neutral toilets not only highlights the needs of a particular group of people (trans and gender-variant people) but also suggests how these signs, and the discourses they represent, accumulate (mistaken/fixed) meaning over time and, most importantly, how these meanings are open to contestation and resistance through the agency of individuals within a culture.

THE POWER OF SIGNS

The sex-segregated nature of the signs most commonly associated with public toilets is reflected in the material world too, with the majority of public toilets adhering to a strict segregation of the sexes. This is a commonly agreed custom both within and across many cultures. In particular, the signs reinforce an **ideological** belief in many cultures that the difference *between* the sexes is much more important than the many ways in which men and women are also similar. Ideology is a contested concept for discourse analysts but is seen by many as central in understanding how meaning is mediated through signs and other communication practices.

For discourse analysts, ideology is inextricably related to ideas of power and is related to Karl Marx's (1818–83) notions about the ways in which the many are controlled through a set of ideas that uniquely serve the interests of a small but dominant elite. Marx's ideas about **false consciousness**, through which people erroneously believe that what they say and do is completely in their own interests, has been dismissed as being overly deterministic. More recent theorists continue to work with the concept of ideology, recognising its link with power, but adopting more nuanced understandings of these concepts. Here, ideology is *not* seen as the opposite of some truth that is held by an elite: according to these approaches, there is not a single 'truth' and therefore neither is there an ideology that could even be identified. Ideology, here, is seen as a fragmented and often contradictory constellation of beliefs that usually parade as 'common sense', which guide the beliefs and activities of groups/cultures, thus shaping an unending powerplay within and across groups/cultures.

Many discourse analysts – and particularly those who identify with Critical Discourse Analysis – adopt and adapt a **Foucauldian** approach that conceptualises power as inextricably linked with knowledge. This conceptualisation is, most often, represented by 'Power/Knowledge'. Here, power is not necessarily something that is exercised over another; that is, it is not necessarily coercive. Nor is it something that is exhaustive in that if you are powerful, then I have less power. Rather power operates in multiple ways, has multiple effects and is always in play in the use of language and other sign systems through which meaning is communicated.

One of the main objectives in conducting discourse analysis is attempting to identify the particular arrangements of power inherent in acts of communication. Here the discourse analyst is interested in *how* signs have particular power effects in culture, paying particular attention to who is served by such effects.

Returning to the sex-differentiated nature of toilets as indicated by the male/female signs, you might try a thought experiment so as to explore how you are implicated in and subject to the ideology of sex segregation as exemplified in the male/female signs. Think about how much effort you make in ensuring that you use the toilet that is designated for the sex to which you identify when in public spaces. Subsequently, think about the potential consequences of finding yourself in a toilet designated for the opposite sex. Additionally, think about your experiences of using those toilets denoted as unisex – available for the use of both men and women. In each case, think about you might feel, or how you have felt in these situations. What feels 'right' or 'wrong' about such an experience? What conscious efforts have you made in feeling comfortable in such spaces? Alternatively, think about what would be at stake in actively transgressing the meaning system inherent in sex-segregated toilet signs and going to the toilet designated for the opposite sex.

In some cases there may be legal and police sanctions imposed on the use of toilets for the opposite sex: this is more actively enforced in some cultural settings than in others. However, it might also be the case that other users will 'police' the segregation and, as importantly, that you yourself are active in enforcing the cultural conventions that are signified by the sex-segregated nature of public toilets through your own use. In your thinking through the situations above, try and go beyond an analysis that assumes there is something 'natural' about the sex segregation of toilet practices. In effect, take a critical approach in your analysis: if you do not already, imagine adopting an oppositional reading position as outlined from Hall described on pp. 43–4 as part of your reflections.

This exploration of toilet signs demonstrate how discrete everyday symbols and language are part of larger discourses and also how they conform to and align with those larger discourses. It also suggests that these representations, as signifiers of larger discourses, can help us to see how our world is structured – often in very taken-for-granted ways – and how those discourses have an effect on how we make sense of ourselves in the world. The idea that discourses 'structure both our sense of reality and our notion of our own identity' (Mills 2004: 13) is explored in greater depth in Chapter 9.

5

DISCOURSE AND METAPHOR

AIMS OF THIS CHAPTER

This chapter will:

- explain what metaphors are and how they work;
- explore the use of metaphor across different domains, including everyday life and digital contexts; and
- provide an extended analysis to illustrate the relationship between metaphor and discourses about organisation.

WHAT IS A METAPHOR?

A metaphor is a **figurative** expression whereby something is described as if it were something else. This definition might make it sound as though metaphorical expressions are a weirdly dislocated form of communication that are likely to be baffling, or the preserve of poets. But the fact is that metaphor is far from an obscure literary device: rather, it is an everyday expressive technique that is increasingly being seen as a fundamental, embedded aspect of language use (Lakoff and Johnson 1980; Lakoff 1987; Ortony 1993; Gibbs 1994; Carter and Goddard 2015). It is also of interest not just to language and literary scholars but also to those in a wide range of academic disciplines including Mathematics, Politics, Law, Art, Psychology and Sociology (Gibbs 2008).

METAPHOR AND SHARED EXPERIENCE

Far from being difficult to understand, metaphors can offer a richness of meaning by making connections with the shared experience of the language users in question. For example, if someone says 'I'm feeling a bit rusty' to describe being out of practice, they are calling on a shared experience of what happens to bits of machinery when they are not used – originally, of course, machinery made of metal left in damp conditions. So in this metaphor, humans are being compared with mechanical objects. A similar connection is being made when we say things like 'I need to recharge my batteries' or 'I need to switch off' with reference to how tired or stressed we feel. These two simple examples illustrate an important aspect of metaphorical reference, which is that the idea of shared experience only works up to a point, because societies change (and, of course, languages differ).

So, both the idea of a rusty metallic machine and the idea of a battery-driven machine with an on/off switch might seem antique to future English speakers used to new and different materials and sources of power. Even current metaphorical expressions where we compare ourselves to computers, such as 'I can't process that' or 'I'm in work mode' or 'I need some downtime', may come to seem quaint in the course of time. However, what all these expressions share is the idea of humans being like machines. Therefore, a basic issue to explore about metaphor is that of its consequences in our thinking and behaviour: to what extent are humans really like machines, and what are the implications of thinking that they are?

A further issue in relation to metaphor is that metaphorical meanings can encode the experiences of some – those who are in a position to articulate meanings and have them accepted – and not those of others, leading to sustained inequalities. This was illustrated in Chapter 3 where the terms 'black' and 'white' were discussed.

Phrases such as 'a black look', 'a black mark', 'whiter than white' and 'a white lie' use colour metaphorically, associating 'black' with negative values and 'white' with positive ones. This is just as metaphorical as thinking of a rose as romantic, or of a heart as symbolising love. More is said about metaphor and representation later in this chapter.

METAPHOR AND LITERARINESS

Studies of metaphor have a long history in Western scholarship, going all the way back to classical Greece and Aristotle's work on rhetoric and speech-making. Different sub-fields of literary scholarship in more recent times have seen metaphor as a central device in literary discourse, sometimes as a defining characteristic of 'literariness'. This has been particularly true of Formalist approaches (i.e. those approaches where a major focus is on how literary texts are constructed), such as the **New Criticism** of mid-twentieth-century America, which has come to dominate how English Literature has been 'schooled' in UK and US educational establishments ever since. For example, in William Empson's influential work of literary criticism, *Seven Types of Ambiguity* (2014 [1930]), metaphor came first in his list of literary devices that are implicated in how different readings of a text are arrived at.

METAPHOR ACROSS ACADEMIC DISCIPLINES

Metaphor analysis can be deployed within any discipline to analyse a particular topic or phenomenon. For example, Gareth Morgan's (1986) classic book *Images of Organization* explores the value of a range of metaphors in helping us understand our conceptualisations of how organisations function and how they are structured. Metaphor analysis is also used to highlight some of the key ideas held as central within a particular discipline. Gibbs' (2008) edited collection demonstrates this tactic across a range of disciplines, showing that the study of metaphor allows scholars to work in inter- and trans-disciplinary ways so that they share and extend knowledge beyond their own specialist areas of study.

METAPHOR AND EVERYDAY LANGUAGE USE

The work of language scholars such as George Lakoff and Raymond Gibbs has offered considerable evidence that metaphor is not simply the province of academic discourse, but of all discourse in its various forms. Lakoff and Johnson (1980) set out a convincing argument that metaphor is not only an everyday **trope** in English, but that there exists a complex network of metaphorical meanings that are inter-related, some of which are elaborated from the physical world. For example, there are **orientational metaphors** that associate upward direction with positive values and downward direction with negative ones ('I'm feeling up today', 'I'm over the moon', 'onward and upward', 'I'm down', 'I'm feeling low', 'I'm on the floor'). The future is seen as in front of us and the past behind, and we move through time facing what is ahead; progress is a forward motion and no-one wants to 'lag behind'. We need to 'catch up' with events and 'get ahead of the game'.

Lakoff and Johnson also refer to **ontological metaphors**, where abstract ideas and feelings are rendered in concrete terms. For example, relationships are often conceived as journeys ('we've come a long way but where is this relationship going?'), the body as a container and strong emotions as combustible material within it ('I just boiled over', 'I blew my top'), and argument as a battle ('She shot my ideas down in flames').

As with the idea referred to previously, of describing humans as machines, metaphors such as those above reinforce each other to create discourses – ways of talking, writing, thinking, behaving – about the topics in question. Repeated uses of certain metaphors normalise a way of thinking and represent people and experiences in ways that, to echo the words of Berger and Luckman from Chapter 3, are 'silently taken for granted'.

The metaphors used in any language will both reflect and construct the values held in that society. For example, an extensive metaphor in English about time is that it is a commodity like money – we can spend time, waste it, invest it in something, gain and lose it, have spare time or be on borrowed time. In a capitalist society where the time of workers is carefully calibrated against wages, and where clocks are given as a traditional retirement gift to mark a worker getting back his/her own time, it is possible to see how this metaphor has grown up. But this isn't to say that there is anything immutable about this representation. We may experience 'time as money' as a reality because that is how society is organised; but there are other ways to think about time.

One way to explore the relationship between metaphor and discourse is to consider some of the varied ways in which a single activity or experience has been represented. For example, teaching (and learning) has been described in many different ways, including metaphors drawing on the postal service (courses are 'delivered' as 'packages'), on food ('consumers' are 'spoon fed' with 'taster' sessions), on organic growth (educational establishments often use logos of seeds and shoots of plants, and talk of learners 'blossoming' and 'thriving'), and on building (learning has 'foundations' and 'building blocks' and 'scaffolding'), to name but a few. Each metaphor will suggest not just that a different activity is taking place, but that teachers and learners are in a particular relationship. For example, being a gardener requires more intervention than delivering a package, and, in turn, constructing a building requires more intervention than being a gardener.

METAPHOR AND DIGITAL COMMUNICATION

A more recent set of metaphors – and one that is still being elaborated – surrounds new forms of communication, particularly **computer-mediated communication** (CMC). At an earlier stage, when new types of electronic communication were in their infancy, there was much speculation about their nature: for example, Laurel (1993) saw computers as a form of theatre space where people performed dramatic roles; Turkle (1995) likened the screen of the computer more to the 'silver screen' of movies. The whole idea of digital 'space' seemed highly metaphorical in the 1990s: Stone (1995) talked of it having 'the architecture of elsewhere'.

Talking in spatial terms now about being online – for example, 'visiting' and 'entering' websites – seems normal and unremarkable, and yet these items of language are still metaphorical. In fact, the whole computer world is one big metaphor, from the 'virtual' office furniture of desktops and files and folders and wastebaskets (or more lately, recycle bins) through the communication systems of email and 'chat' to the metaphors of exploration and navigation that surround web activity (the web being perhaps the biggest metaphor of them all).

The metaphors used to describe CMC tools offer an insight into the role of vested interests in the process of language change; they also show intertextuality at work (referred to in Chapter 2). At the point where computers went from being a specialist technology used within the military to a mass-marketed product designed for ordinary households, there was a need for the companies selling new technologies to make their various tools seem accessible. Naisbitt describes their approach to this problem as 'high tech, high touch':

> High tech/high touch is a formula ... to describe the way we have responded to technology. What happens is that whenever a new technology is introduced into society, there must be a counterbalancing human response – that is, *high touch* – or the technology is rejected. The more high tech, the more high touch.
>
> (Naisbitt 1982: 39)

Examples of this strategy can be seen in the many marketing campaigns that have used the idea that CMC could increase our interpersonal connectivity, allowing us to develop new 'friends' and therefore have more human networks. An early British Telecom campaign used images of the space alien ET to advertise its new communication technologies, suggesting that the products were both space-age and family-friendly (*ET*, short for 'Extra Terrestrial', was a Spielberg movie where a sweet little space alien became a member of an American family; one of his plaintive cries was 'ET phone home'). So it should come as no surprise that telecommunications companies used publicly shared knowledge of existing communication systems to label their new products – for example, 'email' – as an intertextual reference to the postal service. (But note the American English usage of 'mail' rather than 'post' – something the journalist Matthew Engel bitterly resents (Engel 2011).) Email was often marketed as more than just a letter, however. One of the BT ET posters described email as 'the new way to write a phone call'. Copywriters were anxious to position email as a more intimate form of communication than a letter – rather, something where the personal tones of an individual could come across, as they do in the human voice.

One of the results of these marketing campaigns was to meta-phorise not just communication genres, but also language itself. Ortony (1993) talks of language often being metaphorised as a **conduit**, with the idea that we think of ourselves as putting things into language when we speak or write, and think of the receiver of our messages as taking things out. A frequent metaphor of language in new communication contexts is that of 'chat', not in the sense of being actual spoken language but with the meaning of inconse-quential, intimate, fleeting communication, the kind we have with people we know well and trust – warm but trivial exchanges of personal information. Beginning with 'chatrooms' where people went to specific places to have these kinds of conversations, we now have 'chat' tools that are attached not only to most social media sites but also retail sites where friendly service agents are waiting to 'help'. Elaborated in social media contexts where users are encouraged to develop networks of 'friends', 'chat' has evolved into many variants, including multimedia tools such as 'Snapchat' that can have no verbal language at all but simply an image.

A label which originally described a form of interpersonal casual speech between friends has therefore become a metaphor for e-communication of many types, all with the powerful connota-tion of positive human connectivity. This metaphor of language does not encompass notions of permanence, negativity, abuse, connections with complete strangers, having personal information shared with millions of others – all of which are factors that have come into play for users of digital communication networks. A similar claim could be made about Twitter, which conceptualises language as birdsong, something that most humans love to hear.

METAPHOR AND ITS ENTAILMENTS

The previous sections underlined the necessity of attending to the consequences of using particular metaphors: that in using a **source** domain to understand a **target** domain, we should be alive to the extent to which there is correspondence between the elements of the two domains in question. (Note that 'target' refers to the concept that is being talked about, and 'source' refers to the idea or thing that the target is being compared with. So if we say 'love is a drug', then the target (the thing under discussion) is love and the source is a drug.) Examining these different components can tell us a lot about how ideas and experiences are being encoded in any piece of discourse – and therefore in any group that produces the discourse. Those ideas then need to be questioned and scrutinised in some detail to understand what is entailed in using the expression as a whole.

For example, to return to the 'love is a drug' metaphor, is love really the same as a physical addiction? There are clearly physical aspects to the experience of love, but is it best conceived of in this way? If we do think in this way, given that drug addiction requires more and more of the desired substance, and in the process that it shortens lives, and causes poverty, crime and other untold types of damage, what does it say about our view of love?

Any metaphorical expression can be quizzed in this way, including any of the expressions quoted so far – from 'love is a journey' to 'I just boiled over'. For example, does seeing love as a journey mean that you have to have an endpoint in mind? If so, does it mean that a relationship that stays the same is seen as less than adequate? If 'I just boiled over' entails seeing oneself as a container and emotions as liquids, who, or what, is responsible for the spillage? Is there a hole in your container? Do you have too much liquid in your pot? Or is there somebody else at work turning up the heat too high so that – not your fault – there is a loss of control? Getting behind such seemingly trivial expressions – termed 'seeing through language' by Carter and Nash (1990) – is a key skill in discourse analysis but it is also difficult because it requires thinking of alternatives, in effect thinking beyond the frameworks of one's own language (see Chapter 2).

AN EXTENDED EXAMPLE

In the field of organisation studies, Gareth Morgan's (1986) work offers a detailed exploration of how metaphors are used in conceiving management within organisations and how the use of particular metaphors has consequences for how work and workers are treated. His starting point was that metaphors frame particular and partial understandings of social and cultural phenomena; that metaphors always highlight certain interpretations whilst other interpretations are consigned to the background. Recognising the complexity of organisations, Morgan explored a range of metaphors that are prevalent both in understanding organisations and that are used in managing such institutions.

Traditional approaches to management have tended to conceive of organisations as if they were machines made up of interlocking parts that fit neatly together and work in perfect harmony. The machine metaphor gives rise to and frames understandings of organisations as operating in efficient, routine and predictable ways: managers expect to be able to plan, coordinate and control productivity and, thus, to make the organisation more effective and efficient with only small tweaks to its structure. In this classic approach to management – often referred to as **bureaucracy** – individual jobs are 'designed' in precise and highly specialised ways with employees expected to work in cooperative and interdependent ways that simulate how the separate parts of a machine contribute to the final output.

The classic image of this type of organisation is of the assembly line where workers repetitively perform the same task and work at a pace that is dictated wholly by the machinery. The metaphor is evidenced in such everyday language as: 'things are humming along', 'working like a well-oiled machine', 'running like clockwork', 'being a cog in a machine', 'setting the wheels in motion' or having a 'slot' to fill when there is a job vacancy to which the next person must 'fit in'. Morgan argues that in highlighting the machine-like efficiency that is redolent of machinery, the metaphor fails to engage wholly with the entailments of the machine in thinking about and organising collective work. Thus, the less predictable but creative and innovative aspects of people working are seen as problematic rather than an asset to be harnessed for such work activity.

The bureaucratic approach to designing collective work has the potential to dehumanise workers, encouraging them to adopt inflexible attitudes that limit what they see as their responsibility and capability. It also overlooks the expectation that employees should be competitive as they demonstrate their capabilities so as to 'work their way up' within an organisation. The ways of organising work activities associated with this metaphor came under sustained attack over the latter parts of the twentieth century with most contemporary managers and management theorists eschewing the approach. However, many scholars argue that it still operates, at least to some degree, in contemporary organisations.

In contrast to the machine metaphor, Morgan highlights a number of more organic metaphors that are adopted by management theorists and practitioners. These include organisation 'as organism', 'as brain', 'as (sub)culture' and as 'political system'. These metaphors highlight, respectively, different aspects of organising and managing work in collective ways. For example, the 'organisation as organism' metaphor stresses how organisations are part of a wider and complex eco-system and, as such, are seen as 'open-systems' that need to continually adapt to their environment for survival. According to this view of management, organisations need to attend and be responsive to the needs of their customers and suppliers. As organisms, work organisations are in constant competition with each other for scarce resources from their environment to survive – the metaphor relies heavily on ideas of population ecology and **Darwinian** ideas about the survival of the fittest. In contrast to the machine metaphor, this approach to managing work organisations fosters a view that workers are a valuable resource in maintaining the health of the organisation, using their creativity and innovative capabilities to allow the organisation to adapt to its environment.

However, like all metaphors, this one tends to frame and construct partial views of organisations. The organism metaphor tends to over-emphasise the role of an organisation's environment in determining how work is managed; that, unlike organisms in the natural world, work organisations and the 'environments' in which they are located are social constructions. As such, there is often little agreement between organisational members about the nature of the environment and, in any case, many argue that organisations can exert a great deal of control over the environment in which they operate. Equally, this metaphor relies heavily on the idea that organisations, like other organisms, are unified and harmonious systems with all parts working in concert to achieve mutually agreed goals. However, experience of working in and researching organisations highlights the ways in which the politics of organisational life render this view overly simplistic. Additionally, the metaphor fails to recognise that workers are motivated by a diverse range of goals, only some of which may coincide with those of the organisation.

Morgan's analysis of some of the many metaphors applied in thinking about work organisations highlights how metaphors are important **discursive resources** in helping to think and communicate ideas about complex phenomena. He shows how a range of metaphors provide new angles or perspectives from which to view the target of our analysis. In his book he promotes the 'generative function' (Tietze et al. 2003) of metaphor in providing multiple ways of seeing the same phenomena.

In doing so, Morgan heeds the more general advice of cultural analysts who point out that just as metaphorical thinking is productive in getting us to think in creative and innovative ways, we should also be wary of being seduced into thinking that any particular metaphor represents some sort of truth about the target phenomena that we wish to understand.

METAPHORS OF THE FIELD

Gareth Morgan's classic work on metaphor shows how the study of this trope can help us to understand complex institutions. His work also reflects a wider interest in the Social Sciences in recognising that all language – including academic language – is inherently metaphorical, and that this has implications for what is known about the social world. Morgan's book adopts a mixture of **deductive** metaphor analysis – in which a metaphor is applied to evaluate how it helps in understanding a target phenomenon – and a more **inductive** approach which tries to identify the metaphors already in use in a particular context and which influence our ways of thinking and seeing (Mangham 1996). This latter approach has been adopted widely in many Social Science disciplines including organisation studies. Tietze et al. (2003) refer to this approach as 'metaphors of the field'. In effect, the use of metaphors is tracked within an organisation by using ethnographic methods of research, for example by observing interactions, talking to organisational members and examining written communications.

This approach can highlight the repeated use of particular metaphors among organisational members, but might also show the existence of 'counter-metaphors'. The approach is applicable to any organisation in which an individual spends time – for example, a college or university, a workplace, a faith group, an interest group or a community group. The work would involve identifying some of the 'metaphors of the field' in the chosen context, seeing if they recur and exploring what entailments the metaphors-in-use would have for how organisational members see and experience the context. There may also be 'counter-metaphors' in evidence in the everyday communication of members, and it would be revealing to see how these are dealt with in the context.

DEEP AND SURFACE FORMS

Conducting an analysis of the metaphors-in-use within a given context would highlight some of the distinctions made by metaphor analysts. One such distinction is between 'root' or 'deep' and surface metaphors. Root or **deep metaphors** give rise to and link together a number of **surface metaphors**. For example, the 'argument is war' metaphor gives rise to a series of surface metaphors such as 'we called a truce' and 'I was caught in the cross-fire'. Root metaphors reflect deeply embedded cultural understandings of social life, shaping and constraining how we think and act in situations.

Deep metaphors are often highly conventionalised and are so ingrained in their use that we may not even realise we are being metaphorical. For example, we may talk about an expensive purchase as having 'cost an arm and a leg', or refer to 'breaking the ice' when meeting new people. In organisational contexts examples might include 'the head' or 'a branch' of an organisation, referring to employees as 'hands' or 'working your way up' in an organisation. Some argue that such metaphors offer little insight into understanding phenomena because they are so highly conventionalised and therefore come to have fixed meaning. However, those adopting a critical approach to discourse analysis argue that it is precisely these metaphors that should be examined and deconstructed because it is in disrupting such seeming fixity in language that cultural assumptions can be examined and challenged.

In Chapter 3, we referred to the ways in which the colour metaphor of black/white is widely associated with negative and positive connotations. It was precisely in recognising this linguistic phenomenon that the American civil rights movement during the 1960s and 1970s adopted the slogan 'Black is Beautiful' to counter those negative cultural associations that had become ossified over time but continued to have consequences for the ways people of colour were treated in society. In a similar way, the routine metaphors associated with workplace discourse index traditional and ideological ideas about organisational life and how work organisations ought to be structured. Referring to the leader of an organisation as 'the head' signifies a traditional vertical divide in organisations between management and labour with the former associated with the higher-order, 'brain work' of controlling and planning activities.

Management activity was contrasted with the physical work expected of shop–floor labour which, in traditional management discourse, was seen as having much lower value and status. Similarly, the 'working your way up' metaphor evokes the architecture of traditional work spaces with management occupying higher-level spaces than those of workers. Management were often, and literally, placed on higher levels than employees so that they could oversee (think overseer and providing oversight) the activities of those performing work on the shop-floor.

Both sets of metaphors – the **personification** of the organisation as a 'body', with a 'head' and 'hands', and the orientational metaphor of power as 'higher', both physically and in status – signify and legitimise the idea of hierarchy in organisations and the separation of management and labour. The metaphors reflect the cultural dominance of management ideals over those of labour in discourses associated with work organisation. These metaphors trace their lineage to the era of early industrialisation when work organisations were mainly concerned with the mass manufacture of commodities. Large modern organisations as part of a **knowledge economy** are more likely to be engaged in providing high-level professional and technological goods and services where front-line (a military metaphor!) workers are required to perform as autonomous employees with responsibility for managing both themselves and their own work.

As such, contemporary management ideas about the nature of work and the espoused ideals about how employees should be valued holistically have changed dramatically in the last fifty years. However, traditional notions of the differential value of management and labour continue to pervade contemporary work organisations. These traditional ideas about the value of particular work activities map deeper philosophical and cultural distinctions that privilege mind over body, and thinking over doing, and can be 'tracked' through an analysis of the routine metaphors that linger in contemporary discourse and continue to shape contemporary cultural ideals.

6

DISCOURSE AND RHETORIC

AIMS OF THIS CHAPTER

This chapter will:

- explore the origins of rhetoric and our modern-day attitudes to it;
- identify some rhetorical approaches to analysis; and
- look at a practical example of speech-making to explore the relationship between rhetoric and discourse.

THE EMPHASIS OF THIS CHAPTER

Beasley (2009) highlights two broad academic traditions within the US that inform contemporary interest in rhetoric and political discourse. The first of these traditions – termed 'public address scholarship' – is concerned with the inner workings of a speech, analysing how the rhetorical features within a text make it a great speech and how those features best convey the intention of the producer of the text. This rhetorical tradition has much in common with literary criticism and is concerned with the intentions of the speaker or source. Although attention is paid to the persuasive potential of texts, much less consideration is given to the precise effects that rhetoric may have on the audience. In contrast, the second tradition, largely arising from social science scholarship and referred to by Beasley as 'political communication', is much more wholly focused on identifying and measuring the effects and effectiveness of rhetoric. In this second tradition it is the receiver or consumer of rhetoric that is the focus of study.

This chapter draws more on the first of these traditions. Although audiences and the values embedded in their wider cultural contexts are seen in this chapter as important factors in analysing rhetoric, less attention is given to the 'media effects' and 'audience studies' approaches that are more closely aligned with the second tradition. This is because the techniques associated with the analysis of public address, rooted as they are in the writings of Classical Greek scholars, are thought to be less familiar to readers of this book than studies that measure media effects or audience responses.

THE ORIGINS OF RHETORIC

The study of discourse is often seen as a modern practice. But rhetoric, which is in essence about techniques of persuasion and therefore closely connected with discourse, dates back to the philosophical figures of Ancient Greece. The best known of these within the field of rhetoric is Aristotle, largely because his writings were preserved and translated: you can still read his *Art of Rhetoric* which dates from the fourth century BCE.

Aristotle was not the originator of rhetorical studies, but a later summariser of rhetoric's nature. The origins of rhetoric are thought to lie with an earlier field of philosophy called **Sophism**, but few records remain of the rhetorical thinking and arguments of the Sophists. What we have, instead, is a wealth of writing from objectors to the Sophists' rhetorical work, objections that have imbued the modern term 'sophistry' with negative connotations of manipulation and duplicity. Oxford dictionaries define sophistry as 'the use of clever but false arguments, especially with the intention of deceiving', and give many examples from language corpora such as the following:

> Trying to argue that I had benefited in any way from the disaster was pure sophistry.
>
> He went along with this sophistry but his heart wasn't in it.
>
> It must be confessed that there is an air of sophistry about this argument – and I certainly have doubts about its cogency.

Some of the synonyms quoted include 'trickery', 'evasion', 'chicanery', 'fallacy', 'deception' and 'lie'.

It's still possible to observe a connection between the negative profiles of 'sophistry' and 'sophisticated', although in modern English the latter has more positive connotations than the former. 'Sophisticated' often describes something complex and, if a person is being referred to, someone who has a lot of worldly knowledge. However, the Latin root 'sophisticare' originally meant 'to tamper with' or 'adulterate'; and even as late as 1831 the then poet laureate, Robert Southey, used 'sophisticate' to mean 'confuse' or 'mislead':

> Books of casuistry, which sophisticate the understanding and defile the heart.
>
> (From *Sir Thomas More, or, Colloquies on the Progress and Prospects of Society* (1831))

When 'sophistication' is viewed through a negative lens, it can suggest that people or ideas have lost their bearings through becoming divorced from the natural world of simple, honest experience and expression.

SO WAS RHETORIC THE ART OF LYING?

There are many pieces of popular journalism suggesting that rhetoric and reality are polar opposites, using headlines and titles such as 'Texting as an addiction: rhetoric or reality?' But that kind of polarisation is a very simplistic idea. What follows is an attempt to unpick this simple binary and show something of the complexity of this topic.

Toye (2013) sees the Sophists as the first 'self-styled knowledge professionals' – people who sold their expertise in persuasive language techniques at a time when ideas about truth and morality were linked solely with noble birth and privilege. In other words, the Sophists viewed promotional skills as learnable and not part of inherited 'excellence'. This seems like such a modern idea that it appears unremarkable and uncontroversial, but in Ancient Greece critics feared that the use of such knowledge could give practitioners the power to create unrest among the masses.

Our modern-day version of the criticism levelled at the Sophists is probably the idea of 'spin'. The term 'spin' describes an activity – typically carried out by 'spin doctors' – where language is carefully crafted to position a favoured person or idea in the best possible light (and, conversely, an opponent or opposing view in the worst light). Spin is associated with political figures and issues, but the public relations (PR) industry goes much further than this. These days, most organisations, including educational bodies, charities and other establishments that you might not think of as commercial enterprises, have marketing and publicity departments who represent their respective companies to the wider public. And, of course, the skills involved in constructing those representations are seen as teachable and learnable: in a search of the UK-based Universities and Colleges Admissions Service (UCAS) in 2016, over forty universities were offering undergraduate PR courses, and there were 1,931 PR-related courses available for postgraduate study.

People often object to 'spin', especially in the political arena, seeing it as something manipulative and underhand. However, those same people would be unlikely to conceptualise their own language use on social media sites as a form of promotion – in this case, self-promotion. The development of the Internet has extended the idea of promotion to the individual level in that many of us are engaged in daily acts of self-publication on social media sites such as Facebook. Chandler (2006) likens the constant attention we give to our digital output as a kind of symbolic building site where modern identities are permanently 'under construction'. He sees individuals as using techniques of symbolic **bricolage** to tinker with the identity they publish from moment to moment.

The two worlds described here – that of consciously crafted, professional publicity and that of individual, personalised social media posts – are in no sense separate domains. As more and more organisations use social media and digital tools themselves, the idea of individuals communicating their personal experiences can become part of an organisation's **rhetorical strategy**. For example, the UCAS site referred to previously features student bloggers, with a blogger named each month as 'blogger of the month'.

It would be a crude oversimplification to describe all the examples mentioned so far – from political speeches and statements to interpersonal communication, with the commodified social media posts somewhere in between – as simply forms of 'lying'. But each act of promotion, whether corporate promotion or self-promotion, is a rhetorical activity, designed to position the speaker or writer in a certain way, and to establish a relationship with the listener or reader – in other words, to create a sense of mutual reality. Such shared understandings, between the producers and consumers of written or spoken texts, are created through the use and interpretation of particular linguistic conventions that reference shared knowledge of wider cultural discourses.

Rhetorical techniques and skills can equally be seen in an entirely positive light. Instead of seeing them, as critics of rhetoric may do, as a matter of style over substance, they can be viewed as representing a powerful way to communicate a genuinely heartfelt message. If you really believe in something then of course you would like to convince others of the value of your perspective. What better way to do that than to think carefully beforehand about the best possible way to convey your convictions? Toye (2013) comments that if you were forced to defend your innocence in a courtroom, you would want your lawyer to make a passionate plea to the jury on your behalf, rather than simply rehearsing a list of facts.

We can all probably think of examples of powerful speeches we have heard and been moved by, performances that seemed to be as different from 'spin' as they could possibly be. There are also examples you might have heard about or studied, such as the rallying speeches around the French or American revolutions in the eighteenth century; Churchill's exhortations to British citizens during the Second World War; Martin Luther King Jr's 'I have a dream' speech and Nelson Mandela's courtroom speech defending his fight for freedom, both delivered in the 1960s; or the speech given by Princess Diana's brother, Charles Spencer, during her funeral service in 1997. This list may suggest that oratory is a peculiarly male skill, which is certainly not the case. However, there is a question about the way in which certain speeches, and not others, become embedded in mainstream culture. There were and are many powerful speeches by women but they are perhaps less well known – for example, the nineteenth-century speeches of the African-American social activists and abolitionists Sojourner Truth and Harriet Tubman; or the eloquent performances of Susan B. Anthony and Elizabeth Cady Stanton making the case for female voting rights, again in nineteenth-century America.

SPEECHES AND CONTEXTS

Aristotle's definition of rhetorical skill as 'the faculty of observing in any given case the available means of persuasion' reminds us that speeches are an art form that is highly dependent on context. The effectiveness of any speech is not simply about technique. It will be highly reliant on capturing the right moment and tailoring a speech to the nature of any given audience. It will also depend on the medium of delivery. For example, some of Churchill's most memorable speeches were delivered on the radio, the medium at the time that was the most far-reaching in terms of national coverage, and much better suited to Churchill's portentous delivery than any written text would have been. In contrast, Martin Luther King Jr's speech was an address performed visually as well as **orally/aurally**, delivered from a high platform to thousands at a civil rights rally.

In contrast again, Charles Spencer's speech was both public and as-if-private, unfolding in Westminster Abbey but directed at a royal family who had been recently criticised for their public non-appearance. His speech was simultaneously relayed via TV and radio to the wider public, as well as via a public address system outside the abbey, positioning the public as witnesses to his statements. In all these cases, the speech, the moment in time, the performance space and the broadcast medium were all inextricably linked with how the speech was performed. Nowadays we have the technical means to archive and even re-master historical recordings as well as being able to view speeches repeatedly online. This means we have the power to reconfigure the spatio-temporal aspects of the original performances, preserving them in time and sending them across the world for possible repeated viewings. Something originally delivered to an audience of thousands face-to-face can be watched again on a digital device by an individual on a train. The whole notion of time, space and audience in the light of our new communication technologies is therefore profoundly different from that of pre-Internet times.

The audience – or, rather, audiences – for any speech is of course an extremely important aspect of context. Speeches are sometimes likened to monologues because these two types of spoken language both consist of a single speaker. However, it is a mistake to think of speeches as one-sided affairs. Audiences of face-to-face speeches may not be interactive in any conversational sense, but they exert a powerful influence on how a speech proceeds and how a speaker performs. You have only to think about the importance of laughter in response to a speaker's joke, or the importance of applause at the end of a rousing set of statements, to recognise that although audiences might not 'speak' (hecklers do just that, of course), they have a crucial interactive role. To analyse a speech as if it were just a paper-based text is therefore not to analyse a speech at all, but a paper-based representation of one. The relationship between a speech in writing and the original performance is the same as that between a **transcript** of a conversation and the original dialogue, or between a playscript and a dramatic performance, or between the **log** of an online 'chat' and the real-time engagement itself.

ARISTOTLE'S RHETORICAL CATEGORIES AND STRUCTURES

Aristotle outlined three main genres within the field of rhetoric: **forensic**, or courtroom rhetoric, heavily dependent on marshalling factual evidence; **epideictic** rhetoric, which relies on display for its effect (for example, a funeral oration); and **deliberative** rhetoric, where people are persuaded to take a particular course of action.

These categories are clearly not cut and dry. For example, a rhetorical display such as a funeral oration about a controversial political figure could be deliberately staged to trigger a certain kind of public reaction. However, the categories are worth thinking about because they highlight the possible scope of rhetoric, from the more scientific-seeming representations to the rallying cries of public **demagoguery**; and from written arguments to non-verbal communication.

Within any category, Aristotle also saw a number of different possible bases for persuasion: that of **ethos**, or the power that accrues from the reputation of the speaker; that of **pathos**, or the emotional appeal of the communication; and that of **logos**, or the logical reasoning at work in any speech or text. Again, rather than considering these elements in isolation, thinking about how the categories blend together can be a useful exercise.

The idea of character, or public reputation, cannot win an argument on its own – there has to be some substance offered. But facts alone are unlikely to be persuasive: people talk about 'cold hard facts', suggesting that without an emotional connection or appeal, logical reasoning can only get so far. However, these elements in combination – a speaker (or writer) who has a reputation for integrity, a logical reasoned argument and a passionate presentation – can create a very persuasive message.

Figure 6.1 illustrates some of the ideas previously discussed. The photograph is of an art installation called '19240 Shrouds of the Somme', created by Rob Heard. The installation is a physical representation of a fact: that 19,240 Allied soldiers were killed on the first day of the Battle of the Somme, 1 July 1916. Heard's artwork went on display on 1 July 2016, on the centenary of the First World War battle.

Rob Heard's artistic installation gives a physical, three-dimensional expression to a fact that is normally represented as an abstract number. The 19,240 figures, each linked to a real soldier who died, were individually wrapped by the artist and lie in different poses, symbolising individuality among what could seem an undifferentiated, overwhelming mass.

The artwork departs from what we might think of as a traditional piece of rhetoric in being visual rather than verbal, without any spoken language designed to appeal to the heartstrings. Nevertheless, the installation has all the emotional power of a very effective speech, as well as being genuinely informative for those who have no knowledge of the First World War. The status of Rob Heard, too, as an artist, gives him an opportunity to 'speak' via his installation in a public forum – in this case, a large city-centre park in the UK.

As well as seeing the installation as a possible blend of Aristotle's 'ethos', 'pathos' and 'logos', it is worth thinking back to the earlier categories of 'forensic', 'epideictic' and 'deliberative' rhetoric. Heard's art can be seen as combining all three of these areas, being based on

Figure 6.1 An installation called '19240 Shrouds of the Somme' by the artist Rob Heard. The figurines represent the total number of soldiers killed on the first day of the Battle of the Somme, 1 July 1916.

(Rob Heard, reproduced with kind permission)

factual evidence; being a public display; and being a sobering message about the human cost of engaging in warfare – therefore, arguably, encouraging us to resist future proposed conflicts.

THE POWER OF LANGUAGE CHOICES

Verbal language features strongly within rhetorical fields, and, again, Aristotle's work did much to shape the types of language features and structures that analysts have traditionally noted, particularly within formal speeches.

MACRO-LEVEL CHOICES

At a macro level, Aristotle identified five 'canons', or principles, to consider in speech-making:

1 Invention, or discovery

This focuses on the idea of appropriateness: what type of approach will be appropriate for the audience? It also encompasses the idea of what is at stake in making the speech, in the sense of long-term effects. For example, a speech made by a university chancellor on graduation day is addressed primarily to immediate graduates' families and friends, so it needs to be a celebration of the graduates' recent achievements. However, it also acts as an opportunity to promote the university as a place to be respected and admired as a seat of learning. Families and friends will go away with an impression of the organisation, and this potentially communicates much more strongly than any paper prospectus or website.

2 Arrangement

Arrangement is, as it suggests, about the way the material is organised. Classical texts obeyed fairly fixed rules about how to order ideas, starting with an introduction, a factual outline, a proposition, a countering of any opposing arguments and a conclusion. You may see some similarities between this framework and those of academic essays and theses, where traditional templates of this kind are still applied. However, modern speeches have much more scope for innovation and creativity.

The idea of arrangement can also have a wider remit, referring to the arrangement of material beyond a single text or instance. For example, a wedding ceremony typically involves several speeches arranged in a particular order and delivered by significant members of the family (which members are considered significant will vary between cultures). Within each speech, there will also be an expected ordering of material, with each person finishing their speech with an invitation to the next person to speak. Attendees are likely to be thanked, gifts acknowledged, cards perhaps read aloud, jokes and stories told, promises made, compliments paid and so on.

3 Style

Both the university chancellor and the 'best man' at a wedding need to choose the right style of language for the occasion; and this is the case for any speechmaker. Too formal a register can be off-putting and alienating; too informal can seem disrespectful or – if the speaker does not normally use colloquialisms – fake. Audiences are quick to notice speakers who change their accents to seem 'of the people' – for example, by saying 'gonna' instead of 'going to', or 'runnin' instead of 'running'. The linguist Norman Fairclough, working within the field of Critical Discourse Analysis, talks of the increasing 'informalisation' of public discourse (2010). By this, he means that informal registers have become the norm in contexts where language was previously more formal, for example in public broadcast journalism and advertising. He sees a cultural premium put on ideas of 'simplicity of communication' expressing 'common sense values'. However, he is quick to point out that a 'simple' style is still a style, and one that requires a great deal of labour to produce; and also that 'common sense' is still an ideology, not a lack of one.

4 Delivery and

5 Memory

How a speech is delivered is obviously a key factor in its effectiveness. Aristotle's final canon – memory – is bound up in modern times with delivery in some more complicated ways than was the case in classical times. Aristotle cites memory as important because it was considered a key skill in developing a sense of spontaneity in delivery. If ideas and ways of expressing them are committed to memory, then they can be fluently produced to order, but made to seem unrehearsed and therefore genuinely felt. However, modern technologies such as the autocue have removed the need for modern speakers to commit text to memory. At the same time, the use of an autocue in itself requires a particular skill – to read without seeming to. Although we all know that speeches are pre-planned, the more any speech appears to be contrived, the less convincing it will be. Speechmakers want to sound spontaneous without being it.

A wide range of further aspects are involved in the delivery of a speech, from voice pitch and **intonation** to rhythm and speed; from gaze direction and eye contact to facial expression; and from posture and gesture to style of dress. Attention to audience is clearly a key factor, with pauses in delivery for the audience to endorse what is being said. The broadcaster Max Atkinson (1984) was one of the first observers to show systematically how audiences take cues from speakers' intonation patterns to learn when to clap.

Orators are in the business of persuading their audiences through their skilful use of the appropriate rhetorical form in given situations, and in being cognisant of the best way of structuring their arguments. Attention to such aspects of speech-making is, of course, dependent on knowing their audience and what works best for the situation in which they speak about a particular subject. However, to be a successful rhetor one must also have knowledge of the discursive conventions and the wider cultural beliefs of a given community. For example, a university chancellor needs to be confident that promoting the university is consonant with contemporary ideas about educational institutions. Currently, this would mean that he or she would need to recognise that universities operate increasingly on business principles so have to compete for students. This may mean highlighting the benefits of studying at their own institution rather than with one of their competitors (Mayr 2008).

In promoting the university, the chancellor can draw on discourses familiar in more obviously business contexts – buying and selling products, offering services to customers, ideas about market distinctiveness, getting a return on investment – without making this completely explicit. Indeed, knowing what can remain unsaid or what is best left unsaid can be crucial in making a persuasive argument. When analysing a speech it is therefore important to identify the references to the wider cultural understandings and discursive conventions shared by the speaker and his or her audience, including what needs to remain alluded to rather than overtly mentioned.

HOW MUCH OF THE FIVE CANONS CAN BE USED TO REFER TO WRITTEN TEXT?

Much of what has been said so far can also be applied to writing. After all, writers also need to think about appropriateness for their audiences, about how to arrange their material, about the style of their language and – with their physical absence from any immediate face-to-face context – how to replicate some of those key aspects of **prosody**, **paralanguage** and non-verbal behaviour that are present in oral-aural communication. The somewhat disembodied nature of writing presents a particular challenge in real-time communication contexts, or in those where a fast give-and-take of written messages is expected, such as SMS. Digital communicators have to find ways to reshape their writing to capture some of the nuances of meaning inherent in face-to-face dialogue.

Thurlow (2003) showed how texters adapted their written language to help their readers 'hear' their voice – for example, by writing 'wiv' instead of 'with', or 'av' instead of 'have'. Goddard (2005) showed how participants who were new to online writing contexts had to be resourceful in working out how others had intended to sound. For example, Simon and Natalie, below, are engaged in internet 'chat', and Simon is trying to understand what tone of voice Natalie intended when she wrote 'yeah' (initially written as 'yeak', then 'yea'):

```
Natalie>>    yeak
Natalie>>    sorry yea
Simon>>      why yeah
```

Natalie>>	i dont mean it like yeah man I mean it like yeay
Simon>>	what is the difference
Natalie>>	it's happier and less cheesy
Simon>>	and that is worthy of a yehah

Because new forms of writing such as the one exemplified here bring with them some of the pragmatic constraints that we formerly associated with spoken dialogue, they are often referred to as 'hybrids' – blends of spoken and written features.

The extract shows two people discussing how to represent a sound ('yeah') in writing. Given that many aspects of speech are not words in the formal, dictionary-based sense, how to represent spoken language is by no means straightforward. However, this area is not new, despite the new hybrid texts we are producing in modern technological contexts. Creative writers of all kinds, from advertising copywriters to journalists, from poets to writers of comics, and from dramatists to writers of greetings cards use their skills to represent spoken language in writing. There is more about this subject in Chapter 7. Meanwhile, many of the descriptions so far and those to come, focused initially on spoken language, can also be applied to written language in general and, more specifically, to writing that tries to 'sound' spoken.

MICRO-LEVEL CHOICES

Classical rhetoric listed many language features and strategies that were available to speechmakers, including the following.

Metaphor

Metaphor was covered in some detail in the previous chapter. Metaphor can clearly be used as a highly persuasive strategy because it sets up a particular way of thinking, often involving visual imagery. Well-established metaphors can become part of a seemingly 'natural' way of thinking. So to take an example from the previous chapter, if love is metaphorised as a journey, then to say 'we've come to a crossroads in our relationship' seems unremarkable, to the point where many wouldn't even recognise the expression as metaphorical. In this case, we might say that the metaphorical field is persuasive because it is so hidden and natural-seeming.

On the other hand, a metaphorical usage can be startlingly new and can therefore call attention to itself. In this case, it can be persuasive because it jolts us out of our normal routines and make us look at things in a new way. For example, Anthony in Shakespeare's *Anthony and Cleopatra* (Act IV, Scene 12) complains that his former supporters have abandoned him. He makes his complaint by talking about them as 'the hearts that spaniel'd me at heels'. He conceptualises his supporters' hearts (in itself a metaphor standing for loyalty) as dogs – not just any dogs but spaniels, known for their friendly, loyal, companionable nature, and ability to follow orders. 'To spaniel' is not a known verb, so Shakespeare changes a noun to a verb in the process of constructing this metaphor. In reading these lines, you have probably created the kind of image that was intended – of a spaniel trotting along at the heels of its owner.

New metaphors like this one can offer what some linguists call **schema refreshment** (Carter 2004: 85) – a new perception of something familiar, putting ideas together in a new way (people = hearts = spaniels). This can be pleasurable as well as persuasive, and the metaphor described here resembles many others in being an extremely economic use of language. It could be seen as a kind of cognitive shortcut to a new perception, a fresh reality. Metaphor is sometimes referred to as a 'trope', which is a label for figurative language. The term comes from Greek 'trepein', 'to turn', signifying that a word or expression has had its meaning changed from literal usage to something more complex.

Tricolon

This strategy is one of many types of patterning that writers and speakers can use to create memorable messages. **Tricolon** refers to a group of three items. Lists of three seem very common right across different cultural groups, for reasons that are not entirely clear. Here are some well-known examples:

Life, liberty and the pursuit of happiness
(From the USA Declaration of Independence)

Government of the people, by the people, for the people
(Abraham Lincoln, in the Gettysburg Address)

Friends, Romans, Countrymen
(Funeral oratory by Mark Antony about Julius Caesar,
in Shakespeare's *Julius Caesar*)

Blood, sweat and tears
(Attributed to many different speakers)

Location, location, location
(Catchphrase about house-selling and the name
of a UK TV show on the same subject)

Education, education, education
(Spoken by the UK Prime Minister, Tony Blair, when
asked about his government's priorities)

Stop, Look and Listen
(Notice at railway level crossings in the UK)

I came, I saw, I conquered
(Supposedly spoken by Julius Caesar when conquering
Gaul. The original Latin form would have
been veni, vidi, vici)

Hook, line and sinker
(Idiomatic expression taken from fishing, meaning
'completely deceived', for example 'he fell for
the scam, hook, line and sinker')

Lock, stock and barrel
(Another idiom, this time from the parts of a musket gun,
meaning 'everything', for example 'she emptied
the flat, lock, stock and barrel')

On your marks, get set, go
(Starter's orders at the beginning of a race)

One, two, three, go

(Preparing for some joint action, perhaps in lifting
something, or in syncing to music)

Births, marriages and deaths

(A repeated sentence in newspaper listings
and official archives)

There are also many book titles and popular stories that use lists of three: for example, *Goldilocks and the Three Bears*, *The Three Musketeers*, *Three Little Pigs*, *Three Billy Goats Gruff* and *Three Wise Men*.

There has been much speculation about why three items in a list occur so frequently. One suggestion is about memory-load – that a larger number would be more difficult to remember. A list of two hardly seems worth the name 'list'. In speech, a list of three often has a predictable intonation contour, with the first two items carrying raised tones, and the third a falling tone.

Repetition

There are some examples of repetition in the lists of three in the previous section. Repetition is an interesting language strategy because it is not simply a case of a speaker or writer repeating themselves. In fact, we normally expect stylistic variation in the texts that are presented to us, particularly in writing; and we would regard a relative or friend or colleague who repeated themselves a lot in speech as a 'bore' or as 'rambling' (or even as ill). Repetition clearly has to seem intentional and **foregrounded** to be counted as something meaningful: it needs to look like a carefully wrought, deliberate choice.

Looking at the example below is revealing of how repetition can work. The repetition of the word 'people' is clearly central to the statement, referring to the principle of democratic government. However, the repetition serves to highlight the contrasts and different emphases provided by the prepositions 'of', 'by' and 'for'. Repetition as a strategy therefore needs to be considered not as an isolated phenomenon, but as an inextricable part of the wider textual patterns being woven.

Government of the people, by the people, for the people

(Abraham Lincoln, in the Gettysburg Address)

Antithesis

While repetition involves the repeated occurrence of the same, or similar, items, **antithesis** is about contrasts, or opposites. For example, when Neil Armstrong broadcast from space in 1969, he contrasted his walk on the moon's surface with the large-scale scientific developments that the space trip would enable in future years: 'That's one small step for a man, one giant leap for mankind'.

Contrasts are often in evidence in political debate because of its oppositional nature. 'Problems' or 'causes' and 'solutions' are frequently part of political discourse, in expressions such as the following: 'Business must be part of the solution, not part of the problem'. Political speeches may also set up contrasting scenarios because speakers want to identify themselves with a positive polarity – for example, 'light' rather than 'darkness'; 'prosperity' rather than 'poverty'; 'strength' rather than 'weakness'; 'pride' rather than 'shame'.

Parallelism

Parallelism describes structures that echo each other in the structural form they take. As with the other features in this list, the presence of one type of feature doesn't rule out another being in operation at the same time. So, for example, 'easy come, easy go' and 'what goes around, comes around' both employ contrasts of 'come' and 'go' as well as parallelism in structural terms. Many popular idiomatic expressions include parallel structures, for example:

Like father, like son
Penny wise, pound foolish
Keep your friends close and your enemies closer
A trouble shared is a trouble halved

Antimetabole

Antimetabole is a mixture of repetition and parallelism, where words are repeated and structures recur, but the word order is different, for example:

When the going gets tough, the tough get going
I know what I like, and I like what I know

All for one, and one for all
Fail to prepare, prepare to fail

Metadiscourse

Metadiscourse refers to the practice of using language to talk about language. In everyday speech, this is a common phenomenon: for example, people often say things like 'to cut a long story short' or 'not to put too fine a point on it', where they are referring to the language they are using at that very moment.

In speech-making and in written texts, metadiscursive strategies can take a number of forms. They may be as simple as explaining what the text is going to say at the beginning, then at the end, recapping on what has been said. Or there may be particular strategies employed, such as **prolepsis**, which has a meaning in medicine as 'inoculation'. In rhetorical terms, this means anticipating and rebutting an opposing argument upfront. A perfect example would be a courtroom defence lawyer who tells the jury they are going to hear bad things from the prosecution about her client, and not to give credence to what is said. Another specific strategy is **paralipsis**, which claims not to intend mentioning something – which in the process of setting it out is actually then mentioned. For example, if a speaker says 'I am not going to talk about my colleague's poor attendance record', then effectively the topic has been raised.

Rhetorical questions

You may have noticed that both speechmakers and authors of written texts that aim to persuade us, such as advertisements, tend to ask a lot of questions. This seems odd when you think about it, because in both speeches and paper-based written texts, there is no immediate interlocutor – no discourse partner. In fact, **rhetorical questions** are not there to be answered aloud: they are not part of a question–and–answer routine in any conventional sense. Rhetorical questions are so-called because they are asked for their persuasive effect, not because an answer is expected. Actually, the situation is subtler than this, because people who ask rhetorical questions expect you to answer them in a certain way: silently, in your own head. Here are some examples of questions that were used as 'hook' lines in written advertisements. In each case, the question plays on readers' fears that the 'problem' described might be true of their own situation. The 'answer' is then supposedly the solution provided by the product being advertised:

Question	Product being advertised
Thinning hair?	Hair restorer
Not enough hours in the day?	'Energy' drink
Nothing put by for a 'rainy day'?	Savings scheme
Could you work if you were disabled?	Insurance
Age is a fact of life, but why look it?	Moisturiser
Mum, why is Granny coming to live with us?	Pension scheme

Speechmakers use rhetorical questions to raise issues they want the audience to consider. They are used to frame the audience's attention in such a way that there appears only one answer which is already assumed to be known. For example, here is an extract from a speech made by Winston Churchill, later to become the British Prime Minister during the Second World War. In this speech, made in 1934, Churchill raises the question of the dangers of appeasing Hitler and the rising Nazism in Germany. The answer to the question posed is assumed to be 'no':

> At present we lie within a few minutes' striking distance of the French, Dutch and Belgian coasts, and within a few hours of the great aerodromes of Central Europe. We are even within cannon-shot of the Continent.
>
> So close as that! Is it prudent, is it possible, however much we might desire it, to turn our backs upon Europe and ignore whatever may happen there?
>
> (16 November 1934, broadcast, London)

Hyperbole

Hyperbole refers to exaggeration. The English language offers many options for describing things, people, events and issues – there is no single fixed way to represent 'reality'. This means that speakers and writers are able to choose a style and level of formality that they believe will achieve the desired effects on their audience. As with some of the other features listed here, hyperbole can occur in everyday contexts as well as in highly fashioned pieces of communication. For example, comments such as 'I've got millions of things to tell you' or 'that bag weighs a ton!' are hyperbolic, achieving an expressive effect (i.e. expressing the speaker's emotion). The opposite of hyperbole is **litotes**, or understatement, which can also be an effective communication strategy. Litotes is often used for humour, where the obvious difference between something and how it is being described produces a comic effect. For example, President Obama described the experience of travelling in the presidential USA plane, Air Force One, as 'pretty nice'.

Sound symbolism

It may seem odd to talk about the use of sound in written texts, but we need to remember that when we read, we 'hear' language with 'an inner ear'. So it is possible to see **sound symbolism** at work in many written texts, from newspaper headlines to advertising and from literary texts to recipe books. More obviously, sound is an important factor in spoken deliveries. Sound symbolism is not simply about pronunciation, however. It describes the ways sounds are deliberately patterned to suggest certain ideas, often relying on connotations that have been established over time rather than any natural connection between sound and sense. Some key aspects of sound symbolism include onomatopoeia, which refers to the words that 'perform' the sounds they describe (such as boom, thud, crash); alliteration, which describes the grouping of the same or similar initial consonants (such as party people, mighty mouse, slithery snake, rain rattling on the roof); assonance, which refers to relationships between vowel sounds, both in terms of difference (for example, killed cold, hate height) and similarity (song sorrow, bland blanket); and rhyme, referring to sounds that match at the ends of words (moon balloon, fat plait).

We tend to think differently about this area when it occurs in everyday speech, compared with its presence in more consciously created texts. It is often associated with literary works, particularly poetry. But it is an important element of many other types of text, acting rather like the sound effects that accompany film or theatre drama to create an atmosphere. Sound symbolism can make speeches, advertising slogans and news headlines catchy and memorable, as well as forming the basis of popular sayings, riddles, tongue twisters and young children's books and games.

A PRACTICAL EXAMPLE

Perhaps most useful at this stage is to look at an example of a text and think about its analysis. The text below has been chosen because it shows how powerful language choices can be, to direct a point of view, lay out an argument and construct a way of thinking. The text is a famous speech delivered in 1952 in the Mississippi State Legislature, USA, by Noah S. Sweat, the State Representative. Sweat, who went on to become a court judge and law professor, made his speech at a time when alcohol was still formally prohibited in Mississippi. However, the State Legislature collected significant amounts of tax from sales of alcohol, and the more privileged sectors of society drank openly. The behaviour of the legislature towards alcohol consumption was therefore open to charges of hypocrisy. Sweat's speech was delivered in this context and his approach illustrates the complexity of the issue. At the beginning of the speech, Sweat talks of 'taking a stand', but as the speech unfolds, it becomes clear that this 'stand' is in fact to set out the radically different ways of viewing the same topic:

My friends,
I had not intended to discuss this controversial subject at this particular time. However, I want you to know that I do not shun controversy. On the contrary, I will take a stand on any issue at any time, regardless of how fraught with controversy it might be. You have asked me how I feel about whiskey.

(continued)

(continued)

All right, here is how I feel about whiskey.

If when you say whiskey you mean the devil's brew, the poison scourge, the bloody monster, that defiles innocence, dethrones reason, destroys the home, creates misery and poverty, yea, literally takes the bread from the mouths of little children; if you mean the evil drink that topples the Christian man and woman from the pinnacle of righteous, gracious living into the bottomless pit of degradation, and despair, and shame and helplessness, and hopelessness, then certainly I am against it.

But;

If when you say whiskey you mean the oil of conversation, the philosophic wine, the ale that is consumed when good fellows get together, that puts a song in their hearts and laughter on their lips, and the warm glow of contentment in their eyes; if you mean Christmas cheer; if you mean the stimulating drink that puts the spring in the old gentleman's step on a frosty, crispy morning; if you mean the drink which enables a man to magnify his joy, and his happiness, and to forget, if only for a little while, life's great tragedies, and heartaches, and sorrows; if you mean that drink, the sale of which pours into our treasuries untold millions of dollars, which are used to provide tender care for our little crippled children, our blind, our deaf, our dumb, our pitiful aged and infirm; to build highways and hospitals and schools, then certainly I am for it.

Sweat later reported that after the first part of his speech, those who supported the prohibition (the 'drys') cheered and applauded; and that after the second part, those who opposed prohibition (the 'wets') did the same, at which point the 'drys' remained silent. He had clearly succeeded in his aim of showing how a single issue can be viewed in different ways, and how this particular issue was fraught with complexities.

HOW DID THE SPEECH WORK STRUCTURALLY?

Structurally, the speech is quite simple, involving two sets of 'if . . . then' propositions. It basically consists of a list of highly metaphorical descriptions of whiskey on either side of the argument introduced by 'if when you say whiskey you mean'. Some of those 'meanings' of whiskey are then elaborated via **relative clauses**, and those relative clauses appear towards the end of each part of the speech, and become quite lengthy.

In the first part of the speech, whiskey is:

the devil's brew	
the poison scourge	
the bloody monster	(that defiles innocence, dethrones reason, destroys the home, creates misery and poverty, yea, literally takes the bread from the mouths of little children)
the evil drink	(that topples the Christian man and woman from the pinnacle of righteous, gracious living into the bottomless pit of degradation, and despair, and shame and helplessness, and hopelessness)

In the second part of the speech, whiskey is:

the oil of conversation	
the philosophic wine	
the ale	(that is consumed when good fellows get together, that puts a song in their hearts and laughter on their lips, and the warm glow of contentment in their eyes)
Christmas cheer	
the stimulating drink	(that puts the spring in the old gentleman's step on a frosty, crispy morning)
the drink	(which enables a man to magnify his joy, and his happiness, and to forget, if only for a little while, life's great tragedies, and heartaches, and sorrows)
that drink	(the sale of which pours into our treasuries untold millions of dollars, which are used to provide tender care for our little crippled children, our blind, our deaf, our dumb, our pitiful aged and infirm; to build highways and hospitals and schools)

Within these larger structures, language is woven into patterns of different kinds. There are examples of sound symbolism such as alliteration, where a sound is repeated at the beginning of words: for example, defiles . . . dethrones . . . destroys. There are also sound echoes of other kinds, such as where words end in similar ways (for example, misery and poverty, helplessness and hopelessness).

There are different kinds of lists within the repetitions in both parts of the speech. Some words and phrases occur in parallel pairs (for example, misery and poverty; a song in their hearts and laughter on their lips; his joy and his happiness). Others occur in tricolon sequences (for example, life's great tragedies, and heartaches, and sorrows; highways and hospitals and schools).

Both parts of the speech use **semantic** contrasts, where a reference or an image is thrown into relief by being contrasted with its antithesis; and hyperbole is at work throughout. For example, the first part uses Christian references to good and evil, and heaven and hell (the pinnacle of righteous, gracious living, contrasted with the devil's brew and the bottomless pit of degradation). The second part contrasts joy and happiness with tragedies and sorrow. There is also an implied contrast in the 'pouring' of drink with the metaphorical pouring of tax revenue from alcohol sales into the state coffers (the sale of which pours into our treasuries).

Grammatically, the use of **pronouns** forms a further aspect of cohesive patterning, both in terms of repetition and contrast. The 'you' that is used first in 'if you mean' is repeated throughout both parts of the speech, contrasting with the 'I' that concludes each part. But there is also the use of 'our' in the second part of the speech, highlighting the responsibility of all the listeners to care for the vulnerable groups in the community – disabled children, elderly people, the sick – as well as to care about the public services that everyone needs, in the shape of roads and hospitals and schools. This shift of pronoun use changes the idea of difference between 'you' and 'I' into the commonality of 'our'.

Some of the lexical choices in the speech create a formal style, with abstract terms such as 'degradation' and 'despair'. There is an emphasis on extremes of emotion and states of being, from 'joy' and 'innocence' to 'misery' and 'heartache'. At the same time, there are homely images that act as cameos of everyday life that listeners would recognise – the warm glow of companionship, the celebratory Christmas tipple, the fortifying nature of a drink to bolster the spirits of the old gentleman on a winter's day.

TAKING IT FURTHER

Charteris–Black (2013) points out that rhetorical analysis should move beyond the language used within texts to consider the broader social, cultural and political histories that frame it. He follows Wodak's **Discourse-Historical Approach** (DHA), a type of Critical Discourse Analysis (van Dijk 2015). Critical discourse work is concerned with how language use perpetuates discrimination and power inequalities, and actively seeks to change those power differences for the better. DHA specifically attempts to outline how language use is framed by a range of discourse fields that are, themselves, steeped in multiple histories.

The following gives a flavour of how a DHA approach could offer some insights into Sweat's speech. His language choices reflect the then contemporary attitudes in the US to alcohol consumption that were polarised and deeply felt by both sides. The nineteenth century had seen a sharp rise in **Temperance** movements that advocated both socially and politically for either reduced alcohol consumption or total abstinence (Jones 2011). The calls for Temperance were fuelled by a range of individuals and social collectives who were concerned by the effects of excessive drinking. However, these local concerns progressed into wider and national movements.

Rose (1985) shows how the concerns of Temperance movements were closely connected with a range of other socio–political reform movements centred on physical, psychological and moral health – particularly of working-class populations who, it was thought, were feckless and ought not be trusted to know what was in their best interests (Jones 2011). Rose argues that these socio-political movements were linked to wider cultural and political panics about the ability of nations to establish or retain power in an increasingly dynamic geo-political context, and had increasing sway in periods when national sovereignty was under threat. For example, the physical and moral health of a nation's population was particularly pertinent at times of economic expansion where labour supply was considered dangerously low, or when war and other types of national conflict required a supply of healthy combatants or had already depleted the population. The misuse of alcohol – one of a range of social ills – not only threatened the productivity of adults in contributing to national agendas but also put the health of children, the next generation, in jeopardy.

The evocative nature of the rhetoric harnessed by such reform movements is evidenced in the part of Sweat's speech where alcohol was seen as a threat to the well-being not only of individuals but of society more generally. Analysing Sweat's speech using an approach that takes into consideration the wider socio-political and historical contexts allows the analyst to identify and highlight how the rhetoric works as it gains traction through an appeal to attitudes that are ingrained in a number of historical discourses.

THEN AND NOW

A continuation of a DHA approach would entail thinking about contemporary attitudes and seeing how they link with past discourses. The work of Wodak and her colleagues on racism and nationalism does just that: see, for example, analysis of the rise of right-wing populist discourses (Wodak 2015) and contemporary ideas about 'national unity' in the UK (Stoegner and Wodak 2016).

It would be possible to link Sweat's speech on alcohol with an analysis of contemporary attitudes; and we would probably find similarly contradictory stories about alcohol use in modern media texts. On the one hand, alcohol continues to be associated, through medical and health discourses, with disease, addiction, harm and risk (Berridge 2013), and through criminal justice discourses with poverty, crime and disorder. These attitudes are particularly evident in contemporary debates when the focus falls on the alcohol consumption of particular sections of society – the poor, the young and women. Indeed, students are often implicated in sensationalised debates about the horrors of binge and excessive drinking. Significantly, we should note that alcohol retains its status as a legal substance despite calls by experts who argue that the effects of alcohol consumption are equivalent to, or more dramatic than, other illicit substances.

On the other hand, alcohol is associated with recreation, leisure and pleasure, and is often seen as having an almost ritualistic role in the transition of young people into adulthood. It is seen as a vital element in sustaining many urban night-time economies as well as a range of related **cultural industries** and thus contributes to the national economy through tax revenue. These more positive views of alcohol are often propagated by the drinks industry itself in campaigns that assuage concerns over the harmful effects of drinking by advocating 'safer' or 'responsible' drinking. The rhetoric used in many of these campaigns tends to stress that drinkers have a responsibility to regulate their own alcohol consumption, claiming that only a tiny minority fail to do so (Jones 2011). Such rhetorical strategies are consonant with contemporary **neo-liberal** discourses that emphasise individual autonomy and responsibility rather than attending to the macro-level cultural dynamics that regulate individuals' behaviour.

MODERN RHETORICAL STUDIES

It is not within the scope of this book to offer a complete history of rhetorical studies, but it is important to mention the work of a particular theorist because of the influence he has had, especially within American traditions. Kenneth Burke (1897–1993) was essentially a literary theorist but influenced many other fields, principally that of rhetoric. In turn, American rhetorical scholarship in modern times – sometimes referred to as 'New Rhetoric' – has informed the development of Communication Studies in the USA.

Burke's approach was to remind practitioners that when they are analysing texts, they are studying the human use of symbols in the widest sense. He argued that rhetoric is 'rooted in the use of language as a symbolic means of inducing co-operation in beings that by nature respond to symbols'. Emphasising the Aristotelian idea of the need for speakers and writers to establish a relationship with their audience, Burke saw that process less as a simple act of persuasion and more as a process of identification – that the audience has to identify with what is being spoken or written. Burke's concept of 'Dramatism', which sees human action as a drama, involves a number of elements or terms. These are sometimes referred to as the **Dramatistic Pentad**:

- The Act – what was done (i.e. the text itself)
- The Scene – where and when the action took place (where and when the text was produced)
- The Agent – who did it (the speaker, the writer – or the person who appears to be in that role)
- The Agency – how the action was done (the methods used, including the language but also the channel, etc.)
- The Purpose – why the act took place (the aim of the speech or written text)

There are many more details that can be explored in Burke's work, including more about the central role that language plays in constructing realities; see, for example, Burke's *Language as Symbolic Action* (1966). But the pentad itself has been applied in many varied contexts. For example, Rutten (2011) shows how the pentad can be used in understanding students' early experiences of joining university through an analysis of the film *Educating Rita* and exploring students' written reactions to the film. Through his analysis of the opening frames of the film in which Rita enters her professor's office and has an initial conversation, he demonstrates how the location of the action (the Scene) is predominant and highlights the unfamiliarity of this setting for those new to university. This finding was subsequently corroborated by the students who related the film to their own experiences.

Beck (2006) applies the pentad in analysing the real-life stories of women who had traumatic experiences giving birth. Beck's analysis highlights the common finding that new mothers are often dissatisfied with the care they receive during labour and delivery, and that their experience is secondary to the protocols of care as dictated in medical discourses on childbirth. Both studies demonstrate the usefulness of applying Burke's framework to the analysis of communication events in that it offers multiple and sometimes contradictory lenses through which to deal with the ambiguity inherent in language. Burke's framework can offer a very useful starting point for analysis, acting as a reminder to keep the 'big picture' of communication in mind when addressing the finer points of linguistic features.

If you want to try your skills on further speeches, there are many famous speeches on the history.com website. Go to www.history.com/speeches and you will find many different categories to choose from, many with audio accompaniments.

There are also many contemporary speeches archived on the TED website. TED stands for Technology, Entertainment and Design, which was the starting point for the collection in 1984. Since then, many further topics have been included. You can view the talks at www.ted.com.

Meanwhile, the next chapter moves on to discuss the concept of interactivity, which will build on and extend the ideas about spoken discourse covered here.

7

DISCOURSE AND INTERACTIVITY

AIMS OF THIS CHAPTER

This chapter will:

- explore the relationship between individual interactions and discourse as a wider concept;
- provide an overview of some of the approaches traditionally taken to the analysis of talk; and
- show how new technologies are disrupting conventional ideas about spoken and written modes of communication.

'LITTLE D' DISCOURSE AND 'BIG D' DISCOURSES

Chapter 1 explored a range of possible meanings for the term 'discourse', referring to three distinct but related areas:

- spoken language;
- forms of expression within a group, demonstrating shared knowledge; and
- widespread and repeated ways of talking, writing, thinking and behaving and therefore, ultimately, ways of being in the world.

There is an obvious hierarchy of scale in this list: spoken language could refer to a single instance of communication between two people (or even one person talking to him/herself); shared understandings within a group are likely to involve several people; and, for something to cross a whole society, frequent occurrences of repeated patterns in different contexts are required.

Despite this difference of scale, the three aspects are interconnected. Repeated ways of talking, writing, thinking and behaving do not occur spontaneously. Shared meanings, perspectives and values are built up over time through countless single instances of communication; and different groups evolve different discourse conventions and different ways of understanding the world around them. Some groups become more powerful than others and as a result, their meanings may prevail for a time.

Chapter 1 outlined Gee's useful distinction between 'discourse with a little d', which referred to particular instances of communication, and 'Discourses with a capital D', defined as combinations of 'saying-writing-doing-being-valuing-believing'. It is worth repeating the extract quoted in that early chapter to recall how Gee elaborates the two different labels:

> These combinations [i.e. of saying-writing-doing-being-valuing-believing] I will refer to as 'Discourses', with a capital 'D' ('discourse' with a little 'd', I will use for connected stretches of language that make sense, like conversations, stories, reports, arguments, essays; 'discourse' is part of 'Discourse' – 'Discourse' with a big 'D' is always more than just language). Discourses are ways of being in the world, or forms of life which integrate words, acts, values, beliefs, attitudes, social identities, as well as gestures, glances, body positions and clothes.
>
> (Gee 1990: 142)

The relationship between 'little d discourse' and 'big D Discourse' is not just one-way traffic, small to big; there is an equally powerful process going in the opposite direction, with 'big D Discourse' **framing** and determining how we carry out individual instances of 'little d discourse'.

This chapter will outline some of the major approaches that have been taken to the analysis of 'little d discourse' because of its importance as an element in the whole domain of discourse studies. The overall focus of the chapter on interactivity is to enable coverage of types of text beyond speech alone, to think about characteristics that may be shared by other modes of communication. The advent of new forms of communication has made older notions of a binary speech–writing divide redundant, and there is new thinking about how spoken and written systems are blended in many digital formats. The first part of this chapter focuses on speech, with writing and new forms of communication considered after that.

In covering different research fields, the intention is to clarify where different approaches have come from academically, for you to think about how the ideas could be applied to any texts you encounter. The intention is not to suggest that where one approach is used, another cannot be applied. You should feel that you are able to combine the frameworks from any research fields that you read about here or elsewhere to fit your research interests and any data you are planning to collect.

To provide enough detail to be of use, this chapter may, ironically, seem less interactive than the other chapters so far. However, it is hoped that the flavour of the different academic fields is captured well enough to help you navigate what is undoubtedly a complex network of traditions.

INTERACTIVITY AND SPOKEN LANGUAGE

MONOLOGUE AND DIALOGUE

There is a temptation to think of speech-making as a monologic activity, and to draw a distinction between speeches and conversations as a discrete difference between monologue and dialogue. However, while it is true that when someone makes a speech, they are – in theory – given the right to hold the floor while others listen, it is a mistake to think of speeches as simply one-way acts of communication. As was suggested in the previous chapter, speakers will be attending to the signals given by the audience about how the speech is being received, and these signals encompass everything that carries communicative meaning, including facial expressions, eye gaze, physical posture and gestures, and paralinguistic features such as sighing or whispering. Imagine that you are giving a talk and people in your audience are stretching and yawning, looking up to the ceiling and intermittently shaking their heads. You might justifiably feel that they are communicating strongly, despite their not having uttered a single word!

Dialogue can have all these non-verbal features and more. Conversation is a co-production, a joint performance, and there are many ways that both interlocutors play their part in keeping the show on the road. Speakers have a number of strategies for monitoring listeners' level of attention — for example, by using question formats such as 'are you with me?' or 'do you know what I mean?' These features are, unsurprisingly, called **monitoring features**. Meanwhile, listeners can give speakers reinforcements to help them continue, for example by saying 'mm' or 'yeah' or 'right' or 'really?' or 'never!' to show that they are paying attention to the twists and turns of the speaker's utterances. Again, unsurprisingly, expressions such as these are termed **reinforcements**.

A co-production doesn't necessarily mean agreement. A conversation can become very heated and involve participants who become antagonistic or sullen and withdrawn. The point is that whatever happens, any kind of engagement (including silence where there would normally be talk) counts as a co-production because one person's behaviour is a reaction to that of their interlocutor, and both participants are jointly performing their relationship.

CONVERSATION ANALYSIS

The question of how people in general manage conversational discourse has been a central concern in a field of research called **Conversation Analysis**, or CA. CA started as a way of studying Sociology, and its originator, Harvey Sacks, became interested in analysing dialogue as a way to understand how social relationships were enacted. You could see the starting point of CA as a form of micro-sociology, an antidote at the time (the 1970s) to the larger-scale research methods that sought sociological evidence in the form of surveys and mass statistics. It's difficult to know how CA would have developed had its originator lived (Sacks died young, in a car accident) but his collected lectures (Sacks 1995) powerfully show his interest in talk as performance, as 'doing something' or even as 'doing being something', such as 'doing being a friend', or 'doing being ordinary'. A focus on the mechanics of spoken discourse was therefore groundwork in building a picture of how people conducted their social lives and expressed their identities.

Sacks' original work (edited in 1995 by Jefferson) has been continued by his colleagues, who have researched how aspects of talk are managed between participants – for example, the opening routines in telephone calls (Schegloff 1979). An abiding aspect of CA is the idea of **adjacency**, which refers to how cohesion works in speech, often in linked pairs (for example, questions and answers, requests and compliance/refusals, offers and acceptances, mutual greetings, and so on). Elements that are closely related do not necessarily have to occur next to each other in interactions. For example, a question can be followed by an answer but other material may be inserted, without causing participants any communication problems. See below, where the initial question isn't answered until the final utterance:

Tom:	would you like a drink?
Andy:	what's on offer?
Tom:	tea, coffee, water, fruit juice
Andy:	do you have any green tea?
Tom:	yes I think so
Andy:	I'd like a green tea then please

CA approaches have revealed much about the finer nuances of naturally occurring spoken discourse, such as ideas about turn-taking and how speaker turns are managed, how interruptions and overlaps occur, and how speakers move from one topic to the next. The level of detail encouraged in CA transcriptions (summarised usefully on the Leicester University School of Psychology webpage) has done much to deepen understanding of the complexity of speech, with all its 'normal non-fluency' features such as hesitations and false starts as well as the myriad of features that constitute the 'soundtrack' of speech – aspects such as intonation, volume, rhythm and **speech noises**, including laughter. CA analysts use a kind of slogan in the form of the question 'why this here?' (or 'why this now?'), referring to their exploration of why particular language features and strategies are in evidence at particular points in interactions.

However, critics of the CA approach sometimes focus on the way in which its very attention to this type of detail detracts from the larger questions about speakers' contexts and meanings. In fact, proponents of CA claim that they are seeking 'universals' in that they are trying to establish norms of spoken discourse that float free of particular contexts and speakers, including the researcher's own knowledge. The idea is to analyse naturally occurring speech and to be able to comment on how speakers are behaving, with no a priori knowledge of who they are or the circumstances of the dialogue.

This idea is obviously problematic. It is difficult to see how a researcher can collect 'naturally occurring speech' without knowing about the speakers and the context of the interaction in the first place. Even if that were possible, the analyst's own cultural position is bound to have some interpretive weight in how the interaction is understood. In addition, the idea of universals is rather questionable nowadays. Norms of usage are not simply freestanding, but belong to particular groups. Norms can of course be questioned, and departures from norms can be described, but as soon as something is given the status of a norm, it has a special power as a benchmark or standard, with other types of behaviour seen as deviant.

As a very simple illustration of a possible critique, take the interaction between Tom and Andy on the previous page. It was used to illustrate the idea of adjacency relationships in question-and-answer routines. But as you were reading, you will have interpreted the interaction through the filter of your own cultural context and you will have asked yourself some questions, or even asked some questions and answered them for yourself. Who are these two men and why are they meeting up? What type of men are they? Does a 'drink' not involve alcohol? What is green tea and who drinks it? To what extent is this interaction a norm – is this the way everybody would enact this kind of hospitality routine? To 'pure' CA practitioners, questions such as these would not be relevant. But in other fields of scholarship, such questions are key.

INTERACTIONAL SOCIOLINGUISTICS, FRAMING AND FACE

If the project of CA is to discover some generalisable facts about interaction management, then **Interactional Sociolinguistics** starts almost from the opposite pole, drawing on sociological and anthropological traditions to focus on the behaviour of specific communities and contexts. Interactional Sociolinguistics is not a single approach or tradition, including as it does many different strands. However, a unifying factor in all approaches is that speakers are seen as bringing their own cultural assumptions to bear in their spoken discourse, often at the level of implicit assumptions and inferences rather than explicitly articulated views and opinions.

An early contributor to this field and, indeed, a shaper of it was John Gumperz, whose influential work was less concerned with simply describing the words and structures that speakers used, and more concerned with exploring the implications of those choices. This meant – and still means – ranging across sometimes lengthy interactions and highlighting what Gumperz called **contextualisation cues** – discourse signals that show how speakers are understanding the nature of the context they are in, including their relationship with others in the ongoing dialogue.

In *Discourse Strategies* (1982), Gumperz distinguishes his work on interactivity from other types of sociolinguistic research which, he says, suffered from the idea that people's language choices were the result of their social group membership in a static and deterministic way – for example, as a result of their gender, social class or ethnicity. Instead, a focus on discourse strategies defines language as action and speakers as active in orchestrating their performances. Language is seen as an active resource whereby speakers make conversational moves and countermoves to position themselves and others. And interpretive work by analysts is based on both evidence within the interactions and informants' own accounts of their experiences.

Gumperz draws on the work of another influential academic figure, Erving Goffman, in explaining the idea of **contextualisation conventions**:

> Initially we approach the problem of the symbolic significance of linguistic variables by discovering how they contribute to the interpretation of what is being done in the communicative exchange. The hypothesis is that any

utterance can be understood in numerous ways, and that people make decisions about how to interpret a given utterance based on their definition of what is happening at the time of interaction. In other words, they define the interaction in terms of a frame or schema which is identifiable and familiar.

(Goffman 1974)

Here Gumperz is referring to Goffman's work on 'framing', a concept that uses a visual metaphor to describe a linguistic one. The visual metaphor is of a picture frame, where putting a frame around something identifies it as a painting or drawing, setting it apart from whatever is outside the frame (wallpaper, paint, concrete, etc.). In language use, the idea is that speakers give each other clues about how they understand the interaction they are in, thereby drawing an imaginary frame around their interaction and defining it in a particular way.

The easiest example to give is of humour and play. Think of those times when you were using a form of digital communication and you wanted to make sure your interlocutor knew you were joking: you may have added an emoticon or another form of expressive language, to show that your messages needn't be taken too seriously. In acting in this way you were framing your interaction, signalling 'this is play' by offering contextualisation cues. Actually, it would be more accurate to say that you were asking 'is this play?', because technically the person you were communicating with could have refused to play your game, and could have taken your message as a serious one, ignoring your claim. Because communication is an interactive co-production, it takes two to agree on the nature of a communicative event.

Both Gumperz and Goffman were interested in applying their analytical frameworks to real-world problems, and the work of Gumperz in particular on diversity helped to direct the field of interactional sociolinguistic studies towards examinations of power and social inequalities. For example, his early collection of research, *Language and Social Identity* (1983), showed how the operation of inference and discourse conventions within interactions reinforces inequality and the stereotyping of different ethnic groups. This particular collection includes 'conversations' of different kinds – interviews, courtroom transcripts, counselling sessions, business meetings – among many different cultural groups and speakers of different languages in the UK, USA, South East Asia and Canada.

While the general aim of researchers in the field of Interactional Sociolinguistics remains that of exploring how social relationships are enacted by language choices within interactions, earlier ideas about social groups have changed significantly. In his later writings, Gumperz (1996) recognised that there was no easy equation between 'language' and 'culture':

> The assumption that our social world comes segmented into socially discrete internally homogeneous language/culture areas has become increasingly problematic. Cultures are no longer homogeneous and language divisions have become more and more permeable . . . speakers of the same language may find themselves separated by deep cultural gaps, while others who speak distinct languages share the same culture. . . . At the same time group boundaries are rapidly changing and are less sharply marked. We can thus no longer assume that language and culture are co-extensive and shared understandings cannot be taken for granted. The one to one relationship between language and cultural variability must now be seen as an oversimplification.

(1996: 376–7)

Gumperz was writing before any widespread use of the Internet, which has of course further problematised any notion of fixed boundaries of language and culture.

Goffman's concept of framing, articulated primarily in 1974 in *Frame Analysis*, has, like the work of Gumperz on inference, helped to shape the subsequent work of generations of researchers. Because a focus on framing involves exploring speakers' understandings of the type of interaction they are in, Goffman's framework continues to be used in analysing encounters where participants are in particular institutional roles – for example, doctor–patient dialogues or parent–child interactions (see, for example, the research papers in Tannen's (1993) collection, *Framing in Discourse* – this volume also includes work on how speakers enact shifts within interactions, for example when a straightforward encounter turns to play, or when a group interaction involves the teasing of some members but not others). Such complexities of patterning were of particular interest to Goffman, who described changes like these as 'keying', invoking a musical metaphor of change of register. Speakers must be able to signal this change of key to check whether it is an acceptable conversational move, and therefore to be understood.

Goffman was particularly interested in the boundaries between play and so-called 'reality', exploring in some detail the many ways in which members of any society have to recognise the difference. A staged theatrical performance is an obvious example of play – not least because it is actually called that – but Goffman also refers to a range of embedded serious social practices that need to be understood as 'not reality' and keyed as such: for example, a fire drill; a rehearsal by police to practise their response to a terrorist attack; and sporting contests that involve structured versions of physical combat. At the same time, simulations can clearly be mistaken for reality when they are anything but con artists make a living by 'making a play' and convincing others they are authentic, and phishing emails can look very much like the real thing (Goffman's work was, like that of Gumperz, pre-Internet, but he would have had much to say about the complex relationships in the modern world between virtual reality and 'real life').

Goffman's basic model for human interaction was that of a dramatic performance, with individuals managing their own, partly scripted, individual presentations of self – partly scripted because we all approach interactions with at least some sense of how things might proceed. For example, if someone invites you to a party, you will have a rough model of the kinds of things that may be involved – fun, clothes, food, drink, music, talk and so on. On the other hand, if you are invited to a job interview or to present yourself at a police station, then your predicted scenarios are likely to be very different.

Goffman's seminal book *The Presentation of Self in Everyday Life* (1969) outlined his dramaturgical metaphor in some detail. He claimed that while we all know that real life is in fact not a play, it is difficult to say exactly how life and drama differ, especially when the two domains share so much common vocabulary. For example, we talk of 'showing ourselves in the best light', of having 'character' or 'being a real character' or 'acting out of character'; we talk about 'making an entrance' and 'making a scene'; we talk about bad actions by individuals resulting in 'curtains' for them; people are seen as having 'roles' in life; and even the word 'person' (and hence, 'personhood', 'personality') has its etymological origins in drama, referring to a theatrical mask in Ancient Greece and Rome.

Goffman's idea of performance is linked with another of his concepts that many researchers have taken and run with – that of '**face**'. He sees the 'face' that we present to the world as having to be 'managed', and, as with the metaphor of drama, there are many everyday expressions about the idea of face that see life as performed actions – for example, 'saving face', being 'shame-faced', 'putting on a brave face' to the world, 'losing face', not being able to 'face' things or 'face up' to things, 'facing down' a threat, having someone 'in your face'. In contemporary society we now have an additional area of **face management**, in the form of the identity work we do on social media sites such as Facebook.

One of the areas elaborated from Goffman's face theory was that of **politeness**, which refers not simply to everyday forms of etiquette such as saying 'please' and 'thank you', but to more fundamental ideas about the appropriateness of language choices and how they relate to social conventions. 'Face' is seen as a complex phenomenon connected with self-image and self-esteem, where any one individual requires endorsement by others, satisfying the individual's 'positive face needs'; but at the same time, that same person needs to have their 'negative face needs' respected, which is to be left alone and not intruded upon. To break the rules of 'face' is to commit a **face-threatening act**. The most comprehensive initial outline of ideas about face and politeness was that of Brown and Levinson (1987). These ideas have sometimes been taken beyond notions of individual performance and have been used to characterise the social practices of entire ethnic groups. However, there needs to be some caution in doing this, as it can lead to stereotyping.

SPEECH ACTS, CONVERSATIONAL MAXIMS AND PRAGMATICS

The ideas outlined so far have had their origins in the Social Sciences, particularly Sociology. But there are other approaches to discourse analysis that owe more to Philosophy. **Speech Act Theory** grew from the work of philosophers J.L. Austin (1911–60) and John Searle

(1932–) who were interested in the performativity of language use – that using language is, in some respects, the same as doing something. They proposed that words should be seen as acts, setting up a relationship between a speaker and an activity in the world.

Speech act theorists maintain that, providing the words being said are in the appropriate context, utterances are not simply a description or assertion of something, but rather an action in their own right. For example, swearing an oath in a court of law, saying 'I do' (at a wedding ceremony) and saying 'I name this ship' (at a launch) are all meaningful actions, if performed by the right people in the right context. In his book *How To Do Things With Words* (1980), Austin outlined many examples such as these – others include promising, warning, greeting, informing and commanding – terming the words said 'locutionary acts', and the implications of uttering them 'illocutionary acts'.

Explorations of the extent to which words are deeds that commit the user to a course of action may seem a somewhat abstract line of enquiry. However, think about contemporary debates about the nature of virtual language use: is saying something online the same as actually doing something? If someone describes an act of violence and shares it online, is that person acting offensively? If they are, then why do we not hold to account writers of fiction who describe violent events? We say that 'sticks and stones may break my bones, but words can never hurt me', but is that true? We are still engaged in many debates about the status of language use and the extent to which saying something can be viewed as doing something.

Another philosopher who contributed insights into the nature of language and interactivity was H.P. Grice, who explored ideas about the unspoken assumptions that could be said to underlie conversational discourse. He developed a set of **conversational maxims** that, he claimed, acted as basic aims for interlocutors, including the idea that we expect others to tell the truth, to give us the right amount of information and to try to be relevant in what they choose to tell us. Grice maintained that speakers aim for clarity but also for economy, and that effective conversationalists manage to balance these often competing factors. He outlined his maxims in an influential article titled 'Logic and Conversation', grouping them together under the heading of a 'co-operative principle' (Grice 1975).

We can all think of instances where people uttered lies, went into far too much detail or offered too little, or wandered off the topic. Grice's point would be that the fact that we have concepts of what should be done – and epithets such as 'liar', 'windbag', 'gnomic' and 'rambler' for people who break the rules – shows that we do have a sense of ideal speaker behaviour. That doesn't mean that rule-breaking is a simple matter – far from it. Breaking a rule can be a way for a speaker to signal a particular meaning and can be a conscious strategy. For example, someone may deliberately offer less information than normal because he or she wants their interlocutor to pay more attention to them and ask them about what they are thinking or reading. As an instance of this, think about if you have ever felt you were being ignored by someone and said to them 'oh that's so funny!' when reading an article, expecting them to say 'what is?'

The work of Austin, Searle and Grice would now be considered part of the field of Pragmatics, within language study. This field is a wide-ranging one, including further exploration of Grice's 'co-operative principle' in a theoretical framework called Relevance Theory (Sperber and Wilson 1986), where there is less emphasis on the language code itself and more on how participants make inferences. This means there is more exploration of the cognitive processes involved. The starting point of Sperber and Wilson is that speakers focus overwhelmingly on the idea of relevance (and all that can mean in any particular context) to interpret others' utterances.

VARIATION ANALYSIS

This type of discourse analysis has the most purely linguistic origins. The aims of variation studies are, as the name suggests, to trace patterns of variation across groups (synchronic patterns) and through time (diachronic patterns), with a focus on their language use. Classic studies in the past have concentrated on accent and dialect, seeking to explain why different groups might have alternative ways of saying the same thing, or why people might change their language choices over time.

Some classic examples of **variation analysis** can be seen in the work of the American linguist William Labov, who helped to develop the field of Sociolinguistics in the USA. Labov showed how speakers subconsciously vary their accents to achieve what they see as prestigious forms of speech, but the idea of prestige can be complex. Labov coined the phrases **overt prestige** to describe the type of prestige associated with established, official power and **covert prestige** to describe a more hidden status that is associated with figures of resistance or alternative power. Labov's study (1972a) of English speakers who were permanent residents in a tourist area of the USA called Martha's Vineyard showed the operation of covert prestige when he found that some younger members of the community were using types of speech characteristic of much older, traditional speakers who worked in the fishing industry. Labov saw this as the younger speakers expressing their resistance to the commercialisation brought by the influx of large numbers of 'outsiders'.

Variation studies have traditionally focused on spoken language. To give a further example from the work of Labov, in his study (1972b) of the speech of young black Americans, Labov found that speakers seemed to adopt a kind of template when they were telling a story about their own experiences. He termed these spoken genres **natural narratives**, and you can read more about this area in the next chapter, which is devoted to the whole area of narrative.

However, as Schiffrin (1994) noted, Variationist approaches do not have to be constrained within one area of language use. Such approaches can also be successfully applied to written material. For example, think about the many types of everyday written text that exist across a community and that vary between different communities – such as greetings cards, menus, recipes, tickets, certificates, gravestone inscriptions . . . the list is extensive (and includes lists!). Looking at how and why written texts vary is just as revealing of sociocultural factors as the choices that people make in spoken interactions.

INTERACTIVITY AND WRITTEN LANGUAGE

CAN WRITTEN LANGUAGE EVER BE 'INTERACTIVE'?

It may seem odd at first to suggest that written language could be interactive, but if the idea of interactivity is based on the idea of two-way communication rather than communication that occurs in real-time face-to-face contexts, then it may not appear so strange.

Older models of language use sometimes saw language as something that was 'transmitted' from A to B, or saw meaning as contained in language and sent on its way, like a parcel. Ortony (1993) calls this idea a 'conduit metaphor' of language, seeing language as a message-delivery system. In this way of thinking, the 'sender' creates meaning and sends the message on its way, to be unpacked and decoded by the receiver. This sender–receiver model of language was probably influenced by older technologies such as Morse code and other signal systems, where language had literally to be decoded.

A more modern view of language positions the 'receiver' as a much more active participant in meaning-making. Meaning isn't seen as something to be packed into language and then taken out, as if it were a ready-made object. It is, rather, something that is negotiated between participants, regardless of whether we are talking about speakers or writers. Just as speakers bring their own perspectives to any interaction, so readers bring their own perspectives to help them interpret writers' meanings. This means that the same piece of writing may well be interpreted differently by different readers, depending on their experiences and contexts. This whole question of how meanings are negotiated and 'readings' of texts are produced forms the basis of many different academic fields, including Literary Criticism and Media Studies.

In Chapter 2, there was a practical exercise where you were invited to think about a written notice from a hotel bathroom (pp. 14–15). You were asked to consider the following questions:

- Who is communicating with you? Why have they chosen this particular format and placement?
- How would you describe the type of language they are using?
- What type of person is being addressed? Do you feel that it's you? What assumptions are being made about you? How does the text make you feel?
- What does the text want you to do? What is it for?
- Does this text remind you of other texts you have seen? If so, which?

It will be useful to think about these same questions again, but this time to focus on the knowledge you brought to bear in framing your answers. For example, how did you know what type of communication (which genre) this was – had you seen notices of this kind before? If you had, how did this particular notice compare with others you'd seen? When you assessed the language use, what experiences did you base your views on? When you think in this way about the knowledge you brought to your interpretation, you are gaining insights into why contemporary definitions of interactivity in many different academic subjects go beyond speech to encompass not just writing, but texts of all kinds. People viewing an artwork, watching a film or TV programme, or even just looking at a garden are participating as much in creating meaning – in 'having a conversation with a text' – as those having a chat on the phone, or reading a book.

ALL IN THE EYE OF THE BEHOLDER, THEN?

If readers and viewers are active meaning-makers, then is it the case that texts can mean anything that the readers and viewers decide? Not exactly. The writer (or artist or producer) has made some choices, and a text of one kind or another has been produced. That text can be interpreted in different ways, but interpretations need to be connected to what is in the text itself and any analysis has to come back to those features at some point, to provide evidence for any 'reading'.

The practical exercise in Chapter 2 referred to the concepts of narrator and narratee in interpreting the bathroom text. These terms will recur in the next chapter, which focuses on narrative. But they are mentioned again now because they also connect strongly with ideas about interactivity. The term 'narrator' refers to the 'voice' created by a writer to address a reader. Immediately, then, the idea of the narrator is of a language user who is 'talking' to someone – in other words, interacting with another. But who exactly is this other person? In Chapter 2, the term 'narratee' was used to describe the fictional addressee – the persona that seems to be being addressed by the language choices made in the text. This figure can be very different from any real reader: to grasp this idea, think about texts that annoy you with the assumptions they make about who you are and the values you hold. If you can think of an example like that, you are sensing the difference between the constructed narratee figure and yourself, the real reader.

A visual representation can be useful to summarise the communication process that has been outlined so far:

real writer ➔ narrator ➔ TEXT ⬅ narratee ⬅ real reader

Different academic subjects and different types of research project might be more or less interested in the specific parts of this diagram. For example, a Media Studies project researching the question of who reads which publications would want to focus on the real readers, while a project researching how masculinity is portrayed in magazines would be more interested in the relationship between narrators and narratees in the texts in question. Of course, there's nothing (beyond limitations of scope) to stop any researcher from looking both at readership data and a particular set of discourses, such as representations of masculinity.

WRITING THAT REPRESENTS SPEECH

Written texts can appear to address you directly, by asking you questions or giving you orders and thereby simulating familiar conversational routines. They can also contain simulations of person-to-person communication within their own written constraints. More obvious examples of this include comics and graphic novels, where speech bubbles indicate speakers' utterances and thought bubbles suggest their inner thoughts and feelings. Literary texts have a more subtle approach, but one that is still highly contrived. Characters' dialogue in novels can be presented as **direct speech**, using speech marks, **quotative** terms (such as 'he said', 'she replied', 'they asked') and various punctuation marks that indicate how the speech might have been expressed (for example, using question marks, exclamation marks, italics, trailing dots, dashes and so on).

A simple example of direct speech representation could be something like this: *'Is it still raining?' he asked*. Writers can also use indirect speech, where speech is reported (necessarily as a past event, because it is being reported) rather than directly said: *he asked if it was still raining*. There are also 'free' versions of both these strategies, with an absence both of speech marks and quotatives, creating deliberate ambiguity about whose voice is actually being 'heard' and whether it is in fact speech at all, or someone's inner thought process: *Was it still raining?*

The simulated speech within a written text can look very convincing, and analysts sometimes claim that a piece of dialogue is 'realistic', but the truth is that novelistic speech is nothing like the real thing. Real speech is full of hesitations, overlaps, false starts, repetitions, unfinished utterances and many other features that linguists class as 'normal non-fluency' – the normal errors and problems that result from the immediacy and continuous flow of interactive talk, particularly casual speech. In addition, face-to-face speech is highly context-related, so novelists have to work very hard in their simulations to describe all the contextual aspects that surround the dialogue, as well as smoothing out all the irregularities that occur in real interactions (even calling them irregularities is problematic, as it is the novelistic version that is actually irregular in its artificiality).

So far, the discussion has been of obviously fictional worlds, such as novels. But many other types of written text represent speech as part of their communicative strategy. For example, written advertisements often feature images of people 'speaking' to each other, or breaking out of the frame of the advert and 'speaking' as if to readers, directly. There are also many written texts that represent speech but with a more primarily informative purpose. For example, problem–solution discourses such as advice columns and FAQs can feature images of communicators and/or their names, with expressions in speech marks, imitating the kind of interactive question-and-answer routines that are familiar to us from speech.

Where written texts use speech marks it is easy to spot that they are aiming to represent spoken language in some way. But there are also some less obvious strategies that can be used in writing to evoke a sense of spoken language and therefore a personalised feel to a text. Writers can, for example, use regional dialect features to call up a sense of community among readers in a particular region, the sense being that the narrator is 'one of the people'. Colloquial language can be used to the same effect, and this is something that public figures are often accused of – deliberately adopting informal speech styles to seem more down-to-earth and 'just like us'.

Informal language can be simply a matter of vocabulary choice. For example, we saw in Chapter 2 that the bathroom text used the phrase 'nipping out', rather than a more formal equivalent such as 'leaving the room', and it was suggested that this made the narrator seem friendly and chatty. A sense of informality can also be constructed through grammatical choices. Speech and writing vary considerably in their grammatical structures, with speakers able to rely much more on context to communicate meaning, and therefore to use **ellipsis** more extensively than is possible in writing (ellipsis refers to omitting elements that are not needed for utterances to make sense). So, for example, if two people are indoors and one asks the other 'Are you going out?', the response could be 'In a bit'. The person answering the question doesn't have to say 'I am going out in a bit'. In fact, if they replied in that way the response could be deemed over-explicit and therefore conveying a negative attitude.

But why would writers want to tap into readers' memories and experiences of spoken language? Because speech, for most language users, is a significant tool for human connection, and links us not only to our earliest memories of childhood and family life, but also to our everyday activities. So it is a powerful strategy for writers to be able to create a 'voice' that comes off the page and connects with us at a personal level.

However, we now need to think about how these modes of 'speech' and 'writing' work in the light of new technologies, because much has changed over the last twenty years in terms of the communication tools we now have at our disposal. Just thinking briefly about our use of new forms of communication can lead us to question at least two of the statements in the paragraph above: writing is no longer necessarily page-bound, so it doesn't need to 'come off the page'; and many people go through their round of daily activities – including tapping into their interpersonal networks – by writing, not speaking at all.

INTERACTIVITY AND NEW FORMS OF COMMUNICATION

A book on discourse that didn't take account of the many new ways that we can communicate would justifiably be seen as antique.

However, in a small book like this there isn't scope to go into detail about every type of new communication tool. In thinking about discourse the focus needs to be on some of the big questions about the nature of computer-mediated communication (CMC) – that is, communication between human beings via computers. One such big question is how to conceptualise this relatively new form of language use – much of it is composed on keyboards, but is it really like writing? And often we see these new tools called 'interactive media' – what exactly does that mean? Without a good sense of the nature of digital discourse, any discourse analysis of modern communication will be difficult.

MULTIMODALITY

In studies of the language of CMC you will often see the term **'multimodality'** to refer to the idea that new communication tools combine the characteristics of more than one mode, speech being one mode and writing another. In fact, multimodality is nothing new. If you have ever read some writing that has an image alongside it, then you were processing multimodal communication, because you were working out how the visual images and words related to each other as part of an overall message.

But modern digital media has taken multimodality a step further. It may be difficult for some people, particularly younger readers, to grasp the seismic shift that occurred in the nature of written language when it became possible to write in real time. The first widespread use of **synchronous** writing was in the 1980s, with a system called Compuserve. Nowadays, communicators regularly use real-time writing in a wide range of applications, from the 'chat' tools hosted on the websites of commercial companies where potential buyers are assisted with queries, to the friendship-based groups on social media sites such as Facebook and Snapchat.

Early 'chat' applications limited users to a certain number of characters, just as Twitter does at the time of writing, and participants had to physically 'go' to a dedicated 'room' (these terms are in quotation marks because, of course, communicators do not actually go anywhere when they are online). Now, real-time writing tools are integrated alongside other communication systems, and many platforms offer a number of options for being in contact with others in virtual space. While formerly communicators had to make an active effort to go online, and people felt they were either 'online' or 'in real life', advances in broadband capacity mean that for many people there are no clear distinctions between 'on' and 'off' modes: 'real life' exists across a wide range of contexts, digital and otherwise. Digital communication is now threaded through our lives in a seamless way, so that we can move between face-to-face communication and virtual communication without even thinking about making any conscious transitions. Also, with high-quality webcams, face-to-face has expanded its meaning to add digital 'facetime' to shared physical presence. Some would of course argue that electronic face-to-face communication is a form of physical presence anyway. Moreover, the whole question of 'presence' as a concept has variable definitions across academic subject boundaries, with some areas considering it not a shared physical space at all, but an impression of agency or force.

While synchronous (real-time) writing has gone from being a highly restricted medium to a widespread and frequently used mode, new communication tools that started life as asynchronous (not requiring mutual presence, such as email or texting) have acquired quasi-synchronous features, such as indications that one's interlocutor is typing a reply. Also, our expectations of interactivity have become more demanding, so that we often expect replies to messages within a shorter time frame than was previously the case. In his study of his undergraduate students' use of texting, Thurlow (2003) had already noted at that early stage that messages were becoming more dynamic in the sense that texters batted brief messages back and forth in quick succession, as if they were having a real-time conversation.

One of the main issues in analysing new forms of communication from a language perspective is how these new tools compare with more traditional spoken and written genres. Crystal (2001) suggests that we move away completely from ideas about speech and writing in describing CMC because we are dealing with brand new concepts. However, there are many instances where we might want to draw some comparisons because we still learn how to speak and write in conventional ways as well as using digital tools, and it is useful to understand how users' knowledge of one mode helps them in another.

It also seems to be the case that we often transfer the communication practices and strategies from one tool to another.

One of the main problems for analysts is that of labelling and description. It is often claimed that digital writing is 'speech-like' but it is not always clear what that actually means. This idea will be teased out with reference to a practical example.

Below are a few lines of 'online chat' data. Alice, who was nine years old at the time, had her webcam on, but Angela (her great-aunt) didn't. So Angela can see Alice but not the other way round. At the same time, both participants are writing to each other using a 'chat' tool.

After the example below, there are some sub-headings which will focus the discussion on the question of how interactive writing of this kind can be compared with more traditional notions of speech and writing. There is also some consideration of connections between our ideas about new forms of communication and how they are sold to us as products.

Angela:	'elo
Angela:	hey I can see you!
Alice:	be back in half an hour got to hav t
Angela:	what are you having for t?
[Alice is waving]	
Angela:	waving at you too!
Angela:	what is your badge?
Angela:	is it for swimming?
Alice:	roast and we are having lamb and roasted beetroot mmm delicious
Alice:	its a pirates in the carribean one
Angela:	coo lovely! we are having a chicken. . .oh!
Alice:	ok have a good dinner – see you later!

Spontaneous speech unfolds in real time, and so does online chat

There is a fundamental aspect of this writing that resembles a spoken context, and that is the fact that it unfolded in real time, as spontaneous speech does. This isn't obvious when the interaction is written out as a chatlog, but the original participants couldn't predict how the conversation would evolve – they managed the interaction on a moment-by-moment basis. There is turn-taking in the written conversation, as there is in spoken dialogue. But as we will see later, turn-taking in writing is different from what we are used to in speech.

Informal spontaneous speech is sometimes supported by non-verbal signals and online chat sometimes has this facility too

In the example above, one person has a webcam and so can be seen, while the other does not. This conditions some of the language use – for example, when Angela says 'waving at you too' she is expressing verbally what Alice is doing visually. The fact that Alice's badge becomes a topic of conversation is the result of her visibility.

Assessing the tools that communicators have at their disposal has become a part of modern communication because we are often in situations where people have different kinds of provision. This situation can produce what linguists term 'metalanguage' or 'metacommunication' – that is, communicating about the communication itself. When participants on, for example, Skype or FaceTime talk about whether they can see each other, or the quality of pictures or sound, they are using metacommunication. This shows that although they might be able to see each other and therefore simulate a face-to-face speech context, the digitally mediated version is very unlike traditional face-to-face speech in that the quality of the visual aspect cannot be taken for granted.

Young children learn to speak as an implicit part of their development but we have to learn explicitly how to use new communication tools

The example of online chat above shows two participants exploring a communication system that is relatively new to them both. The conscious and explicit learning that we have to do as we constantly replace one digital device with another is very different from the embedded way in which we first learn to speak when we are very young. Think about your own learning strategies for any of the devices you have owned over the past few years – how have you become familiar with their communication potential?

We now think of some forms of speech communication as very 'natural' but historically, they were seen as requiring just as much tuition and expertise as our modern digital systems. For example, early users of phone communication had to be taught explicitly how to manage their interactions. Goddard and Geesin (2011) quote from the world's oldest phone book (an American publication from 1878), where advice was given about how to conduct a conversation in this novel environment:

> Should you wish to speak to another subscriber, you should commence the conversation by saying 'Hulloa!' When you are done talking say 'That is all'. The person spoken to should say 'ok'. While talking, always speak low and distinct, and let the telephone rest lightly against your upper lip, leaving the lower lip and jaw free.

You might think about how you adjusted to the different physical demands of the various phones you have had – for example, the newer 'tablet'-style phone compared with the older 'clamshell' style; or phones with headsets compared with those without.

The discourse structure of the interaction is nothing like speech

How would you explain this line?

> Angela: coo lovely! we are having a chicken. . .oh!

Writing is linear – that is, one thing has to happen after another, rather than a group of things happening simultaneously. Try saying 'hello' to a group of people online, and see how long it takes for everyone to reply. Compare this to saying hello to a group of people in a real room – they can all answer at the same time. Writing takes a long time to produce and turns take a long time to conclude. If turns get missed, then catching up requires a kind of emergency strategy of cramming together the responses to several earlier comments or questions. The line above, then, responds to three previous issues – what Alice is having for dinner, what Angela is having for dinner and what Alice's badge is ('a pirates in the carribean one'). If spoken language was that disordered, we'd be in trouble.

The writing is different from formal standard English, and sometimes simulates spoken language

The data sample was from an informal context where participants feel free to depart from formal written standard English, for example by using variant spellings such as 'elo' for 'hello' and 't' for 'tea'. Such choices are less to do with the communication system per se, and everything to do with the relationship between the users – the choices signal a playfulness and relaxation that can characterise family communication. Written representations of speech noises – for example, 'coo' and 'mmm' – can also be characterised in this way, as they use writing to suggest the spoken voice. The writing is not speech itself, but a representation of it.

A further departure from standard English is the use of ellipsis, which is where a part of an utterance is omitted. In her line 'be back in half an hour got to hav t', Alice omits the subject of the sentence ('*I'll* be back'; '*I've* got to hav'), creating abbreviated forms that imitate the written language of notes and memos.

Language choices spread from one digital context to another

As well as echoing earlier styles of note-making, some of the features of the writing identified above can be seen in other digital contexts where writing is the main form of communication. For example, informal styles used in emails and SMS can often be seen to include variant spellings, speech noises and ellipsis in the form of subject deletion.

Corporate business interests try to persuade us that digital communication is 'friendly' and 'speech-like'

The idea that new forms of communication are 'just like speech' and therefore easy and natural to use has a long history in marketing. For example, early email systems were marketed by BT as 'a new way to write a phone call'. Corporate communication providers want us to feel that the systems they sell us are user-friendly and will help us to interact with others expressively (see Goddard and Geesin 2011). As a result, people can be fooled into thinking that digital interactions are 'speech-like' and personal, when in fact (as they sometimes discover to their cost) they are sending messages to the entire networked world. They can also be persuaded of the opposite: that the world is taking note of them, as in the 'Have Your Say' sections of online newspapers, when in reality their comments are destined to remain archived in a forlorn queue unanswered by any journalist.

Digital interactions can, of course, be informal; but they don't have to be. Angela's conversation with Alice was informal, not because they were online, but because they are part of the same family. New forms of communication are often blamed for making us behave in certain ways when in reality they are simply another way for us to behave.

However, if we are going to make conscious decisions about how to express ourselves, we really need to understand the complexity of digital communication and not think we have done enough just by labelling it either 'speech' or 'writing'. It's both – and neither.

REVISITING 'LITTLE D' DISCOURSE AND 'BIG D' DISCOURSES

This chapter began with a discussion of Gee's idea about how instances of language use ('little d discourse') were part of a greater system of values and beliefs ('big D Discourse'), so it would be appropriate, having just looked at a single example of communication, to think about its relationship with the bigger picture – Discourse with a capital D.

The focus of the previous discussion was on mode because new technologies are forcing researchers to think in fresh ways about how to describe digital language use. But if we move away from that issue and think more generally about the interaction, there are several further 'little d discourse' points that could be made by applying ideas from the approaches to speech analysis outlined earlier. This is in spite of the fact that these approaches were developed long before the digital age.

A 'little d discourse' analysis of the interaction might use some ideas from CA about the structural aspects, most obviously the way the participants try to hold on to adjacency relationships despite the disrupted turn-taking, and the attention paid to managing openings and closings.

Ideas about **pragmatics** and politeness could be explored, as Alice has some noticeable strategies to preserve her aunt's face needs, including setting up a kind of 'holding' statement at the start announcing that she will have to leave the interaction (rather than just logging out or closing the chat window) but will be back later. There are also interesting pragmatic questions about what constitutes **phatic** communication in the participants' culture – the kind of talk that acts as a social lubricant rather than representing serious content.

Interactional Sociolinguistics would emphasise the relationship between language use and the family roles of the participants, with perhaps special attention given to the social knowledge and inferential frameworks brought to the interaction; and Goffman's concept of framing could point to the use by both interlocutors of 'play' signals via their variant spellings, as well as to their metadiscursive strategies for handling the **constraints** of the context, where participants have different levels of access to the communication tools.

Standing back from the interaction and thinking about the part it might play in 'big D Discourse' might lead us to think in more detail about issues of power and the meaning of new technologies in the lives of the participants. Alice is clearly more au fait with the medium, and actually in advance of her aunt in terms of the range of communication tools at her disposal. However, her aunt is probably quicker at typing, which is why she is able to ask three questions in a row, behaving somewhat characteristically of adults when in interactions with children by dominating the dialogue. Alice manages her aunt by answering her questions in a logical order. Focusing on the power on display in this interaction actually shows the young girl to be a skilful communicator – unfazed by the communication constraints, not intimidated by the barrage of questions launched at her and unfailingly polite in showing interest in her aunt while explaining why she needs to leave. Taking a 'big D Discourse' approach could lead us to connect this picture with how the topic of children's use of new forms of communication is represented across society.

In fact it doesn't require much exploration to discover that when children's language use is mentioned in the same frame as new communication tools, the picture is far from positive. Tabloid news media in particular are full of moral panics about technology with reference to children's literacy, their vulnerability, their physical health, their psychological well-being and their social relationships. For example,

Goddard and Geesin (2011) collected a corpus of negative headlines about children and technology, including the following about SMS:

> Text-mad children turning to drink
>
> *(Metro* 2005)

> Texts 'cause more harm than dope'
>
> *(Metro* 2005)

> Text-message spelling in school? Have we gone mad? Why does everything have to be made so easy for children today?
>
> *(Independent* 2008)

> Texting is making English a foreign language
>
> *(The Daily Telegraph* 2009)

At the point these examples were collected, adults were expressing fears that they didn't understand the new forms of communication their children were using and therefore didn't feel in control as parents. A few years later we are in the situation where many older members of society are regular texters, with SMS having been taken up by organisations to communicate about everything from bank overdrafts to dental appointments. More recent moral panics about children and technology have focused on the effects of social media, the addictiveness of gaming and concerns about childhood obesity resulting from sedentary entertainment. However, there are other, more positive discourses about new technologies where employability is concerned, with parents recognising the earning potential of game-designing as a career (Sherwin 2016).

From the above it should be clear that a focus on data does not need to be bounded by questions of structure. It should also have demonstrated that it is possible to connect individual instances of communication with larger, society-wide public discourses in ways that are enriching of both perspectives.

This chapter has focused more on speech because of its obvious connection with interactivity. In the next chapter, which explores narrative, writing takes centre stage.

8

DISCOURSE AND NARRATIVE

AIMS OF THIS CHAPTER

This chapter will:

- begin by outlining some language approaches to narrative, including speech but concentrating on writing as the major focus; and
- continue by broadening its perspective to consider how narratives connect with each other and contribute to discourses of different kinds.

THE CENTRALITY OF NARRATIVE

The concept of narrative has a chapter in its own right because it features in so many different academic disciplines as well as in so many walks of life. Narrative is an everyday social activity in conversations as well as being the bread-and-butter of novelists and playwrights. Narratives play a central role in creating discourses because they are one way of constructing a sense of 'how things are': if we tell certain kinds of stories repeatedly, then they assume a tangible reality and contribute to a recognisable discourse. Thinking about the relationship between narrative and discourse from the wider, discourse perspective can also be helpful: discourse is a larger concept which contains narratives of different kinds, plus other types of text too. For example, discourses about education are likely to contain many stories told by individuals about their schooling, but other types of text such as school league tables and national statistics, inspection reports, and school uniform and equipment will also feature as discourse 'ingredients'.

TELLING A STORY

If you are working in a group situation, use this as an opportunity to tell the others in your group a brief story about your schooldays. It could be something to do with you getting into trouble, or something exciting that happened – anything that you think is worth telling. It doesn't matter how rough and unpolished your story is; this is not an exercise to develop professional storytelling skills. The point is to convey something of the nature of the experience or the event you have selected. The next section will outline some research that used this kind of method as a way of analysing how people typically tell certain kinds of stories.

WILLIAM LABOV'S 'NATURAL NARRATIVES'

Chapter 7 referred to the work of the sociolinguist William Labov, who was interested in how social groups varied in their language use. One of Labov's research methods in collecting language data was to ask informants to relate a real-life story about an occasion when they felt they were in danger. His motivation in asking for stories involving a dramatic event was that speakers would relax and concentrate on providing the details of the story rather than being self-conscious about their language use, resulting in more true-to-life speech data. Although Labov's collection of narratives did not start as a form of research into storytelling, in the process of collecting material he noticed that the stories he was told resembled each other structurally. He concluded that there was an underlying pattern that characterised the narratives told in everyday life, at least in the USA and, it was assumed, in the English-speaking world.

He termed these structures 'natural narratives' to contrast them with the more self-conscious and highly wrought literary forms that had up to that point been seen as the model for storytelling.

Labov suggested that typical spoken narratives are structured via a number of identifiable stages, outlined below. If you did the story-telling exercise, think about the structure of your own stories while you read this framework.

STAGE 1: ABSTRACT

This tells listeners what the story will be about, functioning a bit like a 'trailer' or headline. Sometimes speakers use the abstract as an opportunity to check out whether they have already told their listeners the story, the classic example of which is the 'have you heard the one about . . . ?' preface to a joke. If you did the storytelling exercise, you may have said something like 'right, so this is a story about an accident . . .'.

STAGE 2: ORIENTATION

This is a scene-setting stage, involving a description of who the participants were, where the action took place, when the event occurred, etc.

STAGE 3: COMPLICATION

This is what makes the narrative worth telling – something note-worthy needs to have occurred for the whole structure to be more than a simple run-through of events. A complication is more likely to be a major part of the story if the story involves something dramatic, so it could be argued that the type of story that Labov asked speakers to produce – and this was mirrored in the exercise above – was conducive to the idea of a distinctive or unexpected event. But a story doesn't necessarily need to involve a highly dramatic twist; it could just be a recalling of an experience with a particularly close and vivid focus on something.

STAGE 4: EVALUATION

As the term suggests, this is a rating or assessment of what occurred – for example, how unexpected, shocking, exciting was it?

STAGE 5: RESOLUTION

The function of this stage is to explain what was done to resolve the situation, in the event of a dramatic event or twist; or to conclude or summarise the detailed focus on the highlighted experience.

STAGE 6: CODA

This endpoint brings listeners back out of the **storyworld** and into the present. It may involve a kind of moral or message, setting out what was learnt from the experience.

Not all these stages need to be present, and the ordering of the stages may change. For example, neither the evaluation nor the coda need to be part of the overall structure, and the evaluation could occur in a number of different places.

Labov's work focused on the activity of 'telling a story', as a whole entity or speech event. But stories often occur in spoken language as part of other genres too. For example, a lawyer in court may tell a story to the jury to illustrate an aspect of her client's character; a story could form part of some phatic talk between strangers while waiting for a bus or being served at a supermarket checkout; it could be part of a complaint made to a supplier on the phone; or it could be embedded in a wedding speech aiming to praise or tease the happy couple. In terms of research, a story also doesn't have to arrive all at once, fully formed. For example, a researcher studying the way people tell stories about their lives – in other words, spoken biographies – may need to piece together themes and ideas that are threaded through many different interviews and episodes of talk. Stories can be told in fragments and, like pieces of a jigsaw, have to be assembled by the analyst.

If you were able to do the earlier storytelling exercise, you will already have had a little insight into what it means to trace themes and ideas through frequently told narratives, and how those themes accrue to form discourses. Were there any common themes in the stories you told, for example about bad behaviour or narrow escapes or exciting presents or holidays? Can you explain why you chose the particular focus for your own story, and were there similar rationales across the group? Were there types of stories that you felt would not be appropriate, or that wouldn't work? If you didn't do the exercise, what kinds of school-based stories are you aware of from popular media coverage? Are schools and their students commonly represented in certain ways in the stories that are told about them? We will return to the idea of repeated patterns of narrative representation, thinking particularly about mainstream and marginalised perspectives, later in this chapter.

LITERARY CRITICISM, FORMALISM AND STYLISTICS

Literary Criticism has a long and complex history, and a detailed account of it per se is not possible or even especially relevant here. However, a specific field of criticism that developed in early twentieth-century Russia, termed 'Formalism', produced a legacy of paying particular attention, as the name suggests, to how literary narratives were structured. This school of criticism existed within the larger movement of **structuralist** thinking, and its effects spread beyond canonical literary works to embrace folk tales and other forms of popular narrative, influencing academic work in many countries beyond Russia. Although Formalist scholarship was at its height long ago, and many of its ideas have been challenged or rejected, the work of some figures is still regularly applied in the analysis of modern texts. For example, the work of Vladimir Propp (1892–1970) on the nature of folk tales has been used to explore the narrative structures of many media stories, including the nature of stock film figures such as the 'hero', the 'villain', the 'helper' and so on; the French critic Roland Barthes (1915–80) drew on structuralist approaches to literary texts to reveal the narratives that lie behind the many signs and symbols of consumerist society, such as those found in advertising, and his insights and methods are often cited in the Media Studies field.

The origins of Stylistics lie between Literary Criticism and Linguistics, with a focus on the language of literature. However, more recently the field has broadened its scope to include other types of written text. Stylistics is concerned with language choices and with the difference made to the nature of texts by the choice of one form over another. There are many different aspects of Stylistics that could be explored, but with specific reference to narrative, there are certain structures that merit particular attention. Before outlining those, it is useful to mention the way in which the terms 'story' and 'narrative' are used to refer to different things within Stylistics.

'STORY' AND 'NARRATIVE'

So far, the terms 'story' and 'narrative' have been used interchangeably, but in some academic fields you will see these terms used to describe distinctively different things. In Stylistics, '**story**' refers to the factual, event-based material of the text and 'narrative' to the way the story is told. To have this distinction means that, for example, it's possible to say that several newspapers cover the same 'story' but that their narratives are different because each has its own distinctive 'angle' on the story. In this chapter we will not use this more subtle distinction between 'story' and 'narrative' because we are covering many different academic fields and not just Stylistics, but be aware that other books on this topic may vary.

PRONOUNS AND 'POINT OF VIEW'

One important area often used as an analytical tool within Stylistics is that of **point of view**.

This doesn't carry the ordinary meaning of 'opinion', but refers to the vantage point or angle from which the action and the people in the narrative are being viewed. The term 'point of view' is a metaphor drawn from the visual domain: think about the point of view that is created by the painter of a work of art or by a photographer as a result of their decisions about how to construct the picture. As a viewer, you cannot see from an angle that is not offered to you by the painter or photographer (although you can imagine it, of course). Similarly, the position adopted by the narrator contributes powerfully to how the narrative works.

A major distinction often made by analysts is whether the narrator uses the first-person pronouns 'I' (for singular) or 'we' (for plural), which is termed **first-person point of view**, or whether the narrator uses the third-person pronouns 'he', 'she', 'it' (for singular) and 'they' (for plural), which is termed **third-person point of view**.

First-person point of view is the type of narrative you find in personal accounts, such as autobiographies, some travel writing and some stories of real-life adventure. Novelists may also adopt this kind of voice for their narrator if they want to convey the internal thoughts and feelings of the narrator alone, rather than moving around to offer several perspectives from different characters. This strategy can produce a sense of an intense, personal and intimate connection. But the perspective is limited to what that one narrator knows, so, for example, the narrator cannot tell you what is going to happen in the future, or what is happening in a different place from where they are located. They won't have any personal experience of events that happened before they were born. They can only guess at what other people are thinking, rather in the same way that people do in real-life interactions.

Third-person point of view can produce a very different effect from the first-person choice of pronoun. If autobiography is characterised by first-person narrative point of view, then biography typically uses the third-person option. This means the narrator is talking about the participants and events of the narrative by referring to what 'he', 'she' or 'they' said or did, describing the environment around themselves rather than being directly involved in the action. Novelists who use third-person narrators can give them licence to be all-knowing and all-seeing – this is sometimes described as an **omniscient narrator**. The figure of the narrator is differentiated from the characters participating in the action, and can not only describe them from an external perspective, but can also describe their thoughts and feelings, and reveal to readers what has happened to them in the past or what might be about to confront them in the future. This not only makes the narrator seem very powerful but allows the narratee knowledge that none of the characters have. However, this can all be at the price of a sense of intimacy with the characters. Omniscient narrators can sometimes appear rather distant and aloof.

It will be helpful at this point to exemplify and explore some of these choices in a piece of real narrative. Below is the opening of a novel by William Boyd called *Ordinary Thunderstorms*, published in 2010. As you read the extract, think about the strategies used by Boyd to create the narrative point of view. If you feel it would be helpful, try turning the extract into a first-person narrative: how would the text need to change and what would be gained and lost?

Let us start with the river – all things begin with the river and we shall probably end there, no doubt – but let's wait and see how we go. Soon, in a minute or two, a young man will come and stand by the river's edge, here at Chelsea Bridge, in London.

There he is – look – stepping hesitantly down from a taxi, paying the driver, gazing round him, unthinkingly, glancing over at the bright water (it's a flood tide and the river is unusually high). He's a tall, pale-faced young man, early thirties, even-featured with tired eyes, his short dark hair neatly cut and edged as if fresh from the barber. He is new to the city, a stranger, and his name is Adam Kindred. He has just been interviewed for a job and feels like seeing the river (the interview having been the usual tense encounter, with a lot at stake), answering a vague desire to 'get some air'. The recent interview explains why, beneath his expensive trenchcoat, he is wearing a charcoal-grey suit, a maroon tie with a new white shirt and why he's carrying a glossy solid-looking black briefcase with heavy brass locks and corner trim. He crosses the road, having no idea how his life is about to change in the next few hours – massively, irrevocably – no idea at all.

(© William Boyd, 2010, *Ordinary Thunderstorms*,
reproduced with kind permission of
Bloomsbury Publishing Plc.)

SPATIO-TEMPORAL POINT OF VIEW

If you tried to turn the extract above into a first-person narrative, you will have discovered that however well you articulated Adam Kindred's thoughts, feelings and perceptions, you were unable to convey the bigger picture of the significance of space and time offered in the original. The narrator doesn't simply set the initial action by the River Thames; he or she talks of the river as the beginning and the end of something bigger than simply this young man's interview. There's a sense in the original that the narrator could have chosen any point of Adam's story to begin – and that specific moment in time has been chosen because a massive life-changing event is about to happen to him in the next few hours. In a first-person version of the extract, there is no way that Adam can know anything of this larger context.

Fowler's (1986) exploration of different aspects of narrative viewpoint makes some clear distinctions that have often been followed and usefully applied (for example, see Simpson 1993; 2004). Fowler sees the choice of pronoun used by the narrator as helping to construct a **psychological point of view** because it defines how an internal or external perspective is created, and this perspective sets up a relationship between the narrator and the narratee – the fictional teller and the fictional audience of the text. Fowler refers to the way that space and time are organised in the narrative – seen in the Boyd extract as the significance of the river setting and the reference to a future event – as **spatio-temporal point of view**. References in narratives to space and time are sometimes also called **deictics** in contemporary articles and books. Deixis means 'pointing out' so deictics are language items that point out spaces and times – for example, 'over there', 'in here', 'last week', 'tomorrow'. Fowler sees these different aspects of narrative point of view as constituting an **ideological point of view**; in other words, a particular perspective on human society, with a whole set of beliefs and values embedded in the narrative.

CRITICAL LINGUISTICS

The discussion above focused largely on narrative in fiction but, as has already been suggested throughout this book, texts come in all shapes and sizes and they all have their own way of constructing a sense of reality. The same is true of narratives. It was useful to illustrate point of view by using a piece of published fiction but narratives can be seen in operation way beyond the fiction shelves.

Toolan (2001) describes his work on narrative as **Critical Linguistics**, by which he means an analysis that has a deliberate focus on issues of power and representation, and that attempts to lay bare the ideology that lies behind any narrative. Although he analyses some literary texts, he also shows how news narratives work, focusing on some of the language structures that help to shape the perspectives of readers. Similar work has been done on the language of newspaper stories by academics working within the field of Critical Discourse Analysis (CDA): for example, see Fairclough (2010).

There are many different language items and structures that could be associated with how a story is told – in other words, its narrative orientation. The previous two sections referred to different aspects of point of view, and these can be seen in operation in news headlines and articles every day, playing their part in constructing an ideology. And seemingly trivial language items such as pronouns can be usefully vague in setting up powerful positions. For example, if a newspaper headline uses 'we', it is often unclear who 'we' are: is it the news proprietors and the journalists, or does it include the notional readers, assuming that they all share the paper's values? Equally vague are references to 'us' and 'them', where 'they' might be any group of people who are regarded by the newspaper's owners and editorial team as different from themselves and their readership – as 'other'.

Small features of language such as pronouns can assert power in an insidious way by their seemingly trivial nature, so that we overlook their effect. At the same time, larger structural features can completely change the way events or people are represented, hiding some aspects and foregrounding others. Among these larger structures are grammatical choices, particularly active and passive verb formations, known as **active and passive voice**.

Imagine there is a newspaper story to be told about a public demonstration where soldiers are present and where some members of the public are shot. There are many ways that such a story could be expressed. Look at the five different versions of headlines on the next page:

1   Soldiers shoot demonstrators
2   Demonstrators are shot by soldiers
3   Demonstrators are shot
4   Demonstrators shot
5   The shooting of demonstrators

Each of these versions throws ideological weight in a different direction, assigning blame and accountability differently. Version 1 is an active sentence in that it has a **grammatical subject** at the beginning of the sentence (soldiers) who are carrying out the action described by the verb (shoot). The sentence also has a **grammatical object** (demonstrators), the person, people or thing(s) affected by the action of the verb. In this first version, there is no ambiguity about who is doing what, and the soldiers are named upfront, as the sentence starts, as those responsible for the shooting.

Version 2 also assigns agency to the soldiers but they are not referred to until the end of the headline. In prime position are the demonstrators, in a grammatical structure known as a passive sentence. In a passive structure, the grammatical object moves to the front of the sentence, the verb changes its format, and the subject (the thing or person carrying out the action) moves to the end and becomes an **agent phrase** with 'by' (in this case, 'by soldiers'). This structure relegates the agents of the action to a less prominent position than is the case in Version 1, although they are still blamed for the shooting.

However, in a passive structure, the agentive 'by' phrase can be omitted without making a sentence ungrammatical; and this is what is happening in Version 3. The soldiers have disappeared from view, leaving the demonstrators being shot by persons unknown. Version 4 is even more minimal, with some ambiguity possible because the verb 'shot' without its passive (+ are) could now appear as if it were an active verb, with demonstrators as the subject: in other words, the demonstrators themselves are shooting people.

Version 5 is termed a **nominalisation** in linguistics, which describes a process by which verbs are turned into nouns: the verb 'shoot' becomes the noun phrase 'the shooting (of)'. The effect of this is to turn an activity into a 'thing', making the whole expression more static and, because the structure becomes more complex in the process, creating a more formal effect. In Version 5, it's the shooting that's the foregrounded item, seeming almost as if it 'belonged' to the demonstrators rather than being an act of violence done to them.

There can of course be entirely laudable reasons why a news narrative might want to be vague about who is responsible for an action: for example, it may be genuinely unclear how events unfolded. However, when certain representations are repeated time and time again, and when a particular angle is taken on topics, highlighting some aspects and downplaying others, then the choice of language structures is no mere accident or simple stylistic preference.

The examples given are a single instance of language choices, and an invented context. But the instance serves to illustrate how tools of language analysis – including grammatical structures as well as choices of vocabulary – can be employed to explore ideological positions set up by writers of narrative. Writers may or may not be aware of their own choices, because they may be unconsciously articulating the norms and values of the wider culture they have imbibed as part of their socialisation; but in ventriloquising that same culture, they create it afresh by the way they communicate. A good example of this circular process is Kate Clark's (1998) exploration of what she terms 'the linguistics of blame' in the tabloid news reporting of crimes of sexual violence. From a wider perspective, Stuart Hall's (1932–2014) work as a cultural theorist, and that of other scholars who helped to shape the Cultural Studies field, often focused on news media, and particularly the language within it, to reveal patterns of representation that enabled powerful groups within society to maintain their positions.

As should be clear from the coverage so far in this chapter, exploration of the language of narratives crosses a number of disciplines. But there is no single analytical toolkit that can operate in a one-size-fits-all approach. What is shared by disciplines that focus on narrative is a commitment to analysing not just what they say, but how they say it. Whatever mix of analytical tools is chosen needs to match the task in hand.

LIFE-WRITING

Written narratives do not just exist in public domains such as the mass media. Individuals also write personal narratives, recording their thoughts, feelings and experiences in formats such as blogs and diaries. These can also be analysed to investigate how individuals represent themselves in relation to the world around them. The sections that follow will address some of the ways that such written pieces can be approached.

A PERSONAL WRITTEN NARRATIVE

Below is an extract from a narrative that was written by an academic called Guy about one of his earliest memories from childhood. Guy is out with his mother and they bump into one of Guy's primary school teachers (Mrs Clarke). Guy's family live on a farm in rural Donegal, in the Irish Republic. He recalls the social awkwardness of this memory, then goes on to describe his later education, including his entry into higher education. As you read the narrative, use any of the tools outlined so far (for example, pronouns and point of view; spatio-temporal aspects) to think about the language choices the writer has made:

"He's very B-R-A-I-N-Y" Mrs Clarke spelt out. "Oh! Well . . ." demurred the mother, allowing the conversation to happen while adjusting the fake black patent leather handbag awkwardly on her forearm. Its ungainly hang and the stiff, jerky readjustments underlined her flusteredness in this dressed-up conversation.

Perhaps they also spoke to how much more accustomed her hands were to milking cows, carrying buckets of animal feed and the multitude of other labours that filled her days as she kept the small subsistence farm afloat, cared for her eight children and supported her husband who had been maimed in a work accident several years earlier, and would die prematurely only half a dozen years later. Hers were hands that had little practice in the fineries of what even this poor rural hinterland considered posh womanliness. And yet, despite her discomfort and the flush in her face that couldn't just be explained by the afternoon sun, the teacher's comment seemed to smooth out some of the worries, worn with little thought, on the angled peasant planes of her face. Scuttling reverentially away she allowed herself, fleetingly, to nurture the inkling that her five year old might just be different from his brothers. She knew it wasn't good to dwell or get above your station in life. But maybe, just maybe, there'd be a priest in the family at last. The thought, a down feather of impossible hope, glided in the melee of everyday busyness and fractured on the clasp of the handbag as she fished for the entrance tickets that left just enough change for ice-creams. Sure, it wasn't often she and the weans got out.

It was a Holy day. The Feast of the Assumption. The scorching heat, summer of 1976, was already in the record books. I was one of the well-behaved brood dangling precariously from the pram – new in the 1940s – that my mother pushed over the rutted community field to watch the annual horse-racing event.

The memory of that day cuts deep in my psyche when I think about how my life has turned out. Although I flirted with the idea of the seminary during my teenage years – it was one sure way of getting a sponsored university education for someone from a poor, Irish Catholic background – I was never convinced that I was cut out for the cloth, and was truly doubtful that I could live up to the life-style habits that the Church imposed on its clergy. In the end though, I did study at university and have subsequently worked as an academic for more than twenty years.

University was both exhilarating and life-enhancing. It afforded me the opportunity to establish a sense of independence: away from the people, places and familiarities that had nurtured and constrained me in equal measure. I embraced all that was novel. The strangeness of the new was itself part of the thrill, and I soon realised that I relished the sense of 'making it up' as I went along. I was a new me without all the drag of my history and connections. People were willing to accept me at face value, to applaud and support what I wanted to achieve as long as I delivered the goods. No one warned me about going beyond my station based on their knowledge of me and mine. So, I can honestly say that university has opened up a whole new life-world for me.

LANGUAGE STRATEGIES USED IN THE STORY

If we start the analysis with looking at how the text works from a stylistic point of view, we might think about who the narrator of the story is – what kind of person is addressing us, and what that person assumes about us as narratees. This would mean thinking about narrative point of view as outlined previously – that is, the vantage point or angle from which the action and the people in the text are being viewed.

The beginning of the text uses a 'third-person narrator', so rather than using 'I', the voice uses third-person pronouns – 'he', 'she', 'it', 'they' and all their associated forms such as 'his', 'her', 'himself', 'herself' etc. – to describe the world around them. Third-person narration continues until midway through the second paragraph, when first-person narration takes over. This continues until the end of the extract. The shift from third to first-person narrative reflects a change in the relationship between narrator and narratee because the apparently detached observer of events in the first part of the extract turns into a more delineated, personalised figure in the second half, allowing us into his inner thoughts and feelings about his experiences.

This is not the end of the story about narrative point of view, however. It may look as though the choice between third-person pronoun use (he, she, it, they) and first person (I, we) is a simple binary distinction between external and internal perspectives, but there is much more to say. It's important to look at how other language choices in the text work alongside the pronoun choice to construct certain types of narrator. Look at the first section again:

"He's very B-R-A-I-N-Y" Mrs Clarke spelt out. "Oh! Well . . ." demurred the mother, allowing the conversation to happen while adjusting the fake black patent leather handbag awkwardly on her forearm. Its ungainly hang and the stiff, jerky readjustments underlined her flusteredness in this dressed-up conversation.

Perhaps they also spoke to how much more accustomed her hands were to milking cows, carrying buckets of animal feed and the multitude of other labours that filled her days as she kept the small subsistence farm afloat, cared for her eight children and supported her husband who had been maimed in a work accident several years earlier, and would die prematurely only half a dozen years later. Hers were hands that had little practice in the fineries of what even this poor rural hinterland considered posh womanliness. And yet, despite her discomfort and the flush in her face that couldn't just be explained by the afternoon sun, the teacher's comment seemed to smooth out some of the worries, worn with little thought, on the angled peasant planes of her face. Scuttling reverentially away she allowed herself, fleetingly, to nurture the inkling that her five year old might just be different from his brothers. She knew it wasn't good to dwell or get above your station in life. But maybe, just maybe, there'd be a priest in the family at last. The thought, a down feather of impossible hope, glided in the melee of everyday busyness and fractured on the clasp of the handbag as she fished for the entrance tickets that left just enough change for ice-creams. Sure, it wasn't often she and the weans got out.

Although this is a third-person narrator and therefore in theory someone looking on while other people act and react, the language choices of the narrator are in no sense neutral or simply descriptive: for example, the adjective 'fake' in the description 'fake black patent leather handbag' suggests this is not a fashion choice but a result of hardship. The description might seem rather snobbish until we are told that the conversation is 'dressed-up' – false and unnatural, like the fake leather handbag. It is not the woman who is being critically viewed, but the awkwardness of the social engagement – a working-class mother meeting her son's teacher, the latter being a figure of high status in the society of the time. So the narrative voice is sympathetic to the mother's self-consciousness in this unnatural environment. The main point to grasp, then, is that the narrative voice is a highly evaluative one, and not simply an externalised commentary.

In terms of space and time, the third-person narrator is also a complex construction. If you liken the visual perspective to a camera lens, the narration starts very up-close and personal. If this were a film, rather than seeing the interaction from afar and then homing in on the figures, this narrator hovers around the teacher's face and the mother's handbag, perhaps even feeling the handbag's movement as well as seeing it. But then that same narrator takes us out across rural land to cowsheds and farm labour. The third-person narrative time frame is even more complex. We go from the present encounter to the mother's past days – both immediately past, in terms of the shape of her days, and also further back in time, when her husband was injured. We then go to future time, when her husband dies. As the extract continues, after a brief excursion into a possible future within the mother's dreams for her child, we then come back to the present before shifting more radically into the past tense as the first-person adult narrative takes over and looks back at this childhood event from outside the storyworld completely.

The third-person narrative perspective also raises some interesting questions about whose thoughts and feelings, as well as whose utterances – spoken aloud or in a form of 'inner speech' – are being presented.

The initial paragraph of the extract starts with some direct speech, where the teacher comically spells out the word 'brainy' as if it were a taboo subject, or something that might, like the scenario where dogs have 'walkies' spelled out over their heads, generate too much excitement if understood. Because this is right at the start of the extract, it's unclear why cleverness should have to be referred to in hushed tones but as the story proceeds, we understand more about the cultural constraints of this rural community. We learn about these not through the narrator's direct account, but via the inner thoughts of the female character – for example, 'she knew it wasn't good to dwell or get above your station in life'. This same third-person narrator, then, has managed to move from the teacher's direct speech into the inside of the mother's head, articulating her thoughts and also seeming to capture her speech style with the **non-standard free indirect speech** 'sure, it wasn't often she and the weans got out', this being a representation of an Irish regional variety of English.

A narrator who can 'inhabit' different characters' heads, as well as being able to move around in space and time, was referred to previously as an 'omniscient narrator', the term 'omniscient' meaning 'all-knowing'. This type of narrator allows multiple perspectives, including flashbacks and flashforwards, enabling readers to get insights into the complexities of social lives and relationships. In contrast, although a first-person narrative can allow a personalised, individual view of the world, it does not allow the narrator to escape the boundaries of their own experiences and vision.

So if the first part of the text had used a first-person narrator in the form of the child, it would have been much more difficult to give the mother's background and impossible to give her inner thoughts and feelings – these would have had to be inferred entirely from her behaviour, from showing us rather than telling us. Events in the future, or before the child was born, would also be inaccessible. For example, the child wouldn't know that his father would die six years later.

If you want to continue to explore first and third-person perspectives, try re-writing the first part of the text from the child's perspective and/or from that of the teacher.

FAMILIAR CULTURAL NARRATIVES

So far the focus has been on how the narrative has been put together – how it has been crafted. It is a highly crafted piece and, to that extent, it can be approached much in the same way as the extract from the published novel examined earlier (William Boyd's *Ordinary Thunderstorms*). But there is more to say about both these pieces of writing than just their crafting techniques, important as those are. Both the texts have themes, focusing on particular areas of experience or walks of life, within which their 'characters' function. The life-writing extract focuses on a theme which will be familiar to many people – the transformative power of education.

The story is told in a fairly conventional way with an identifiable beginning (someone from a lower-class background), middle (who toys with the idea of getting a university education and experiences the anonymity that university life can bring) and end (whose subsequent success is a function of completing and doing well at university). The story will be particularly familiar to those from a former generation where accessing university education was not as certain and common as it is currently in many developed national contexts. Equally, some sense of the story may resonate for those from particular social class backgrounds who are the first to go to university and/or those from countries where access to university education is less guaranteed. Overall, the story reflects a well-worn **cultural narrative** about the value of higher education and its role in affording upward social mobility. It also draws on ideas and ideals about jobs and careers – that university education provides the best route to professional and high-status jobs as well as guaranteeing progress within particular career structures.

ALTERNATIVE EMPHASES

Notably, the action of the story is organised mostly in chronological order, with early memories preceding those told about later in time. The story could have been organised in a host of alternative ways. In telling about an aspect of life, it is not always easy to identify a beginning. Here the story might have begun with the writer's memories of being taught to read and write by an older sister long before starting school, or it might have begun with another story of being fifteen, getting a summer job and deciding to postpone paid employment for as long as possible. These alternative story fragments could provide equally plausible motivations for attending university. However, all of these alternatives conform to a central trope in Western culture, reinforced in conventional story plotlines, that there is an easily identifiable and linear 'cause-and-effect' relation between events and those that precede them. This dominant ideal tends to sensationalise those events that are considered random, in the sense that they do not have an identifiable and simple causal explanation.

In the same way, the middle and ending of this story might take different forms and include very different details. For example, there might have been a more explicit focus on the way a university education has undoubtedly provided access to a very different lifestyle and set of opportunities for the writer in comparison with those of his parents (the writer became a university academic and continues to be so).

A different emphasis again might have had the writer representing his educational trajectory in a negative way. There might have been a focus on obstacles to overcome and struggles to achieve access. But a story shaped in this way is also a familiar trope: characters typically cannot achieve their dreams without overcoming difficulties en route.

Whatever the shape of the narrative, one of the strengths of narrative inquiry as a research method is that it affords a focus on lived experience – the rich detail of experience that is different in kind from the types of **quantitative research** seeking 'facts' about social phenomena that are generalisable across different populations.

MARGINALISED STORIES

What if the life-writing extract about going to university ended like this:

> And yet . . . my escapes from territories known, and my subsequent encounter with new situations, were, at exactly the same time, overshadowed by the constant feeling of how different I and my background were. I could never quite shift the constant nag that I was out of place, perhaps even a fraud.

Such an 'oppositional' story is one that is redolent of a number of scholars who identify themselves as atypical and therefore marginal within the academy. Many feminist and **postcolonial** writers who identify the academy as an institution dominated by the values and methods of white middle-class men have outlined experiences of being in university settings which render females and ethnically non-white academics as peripheral. Similarly, some working-class academics have been critical of the positions afforded them within a largely middle-class academy. For example, Berube (1996) charted the conflicts inherent for him as a working-class male in becoming an academic. He suggests that in the Canadian and rural working poor milieu in which he grew up, boys with an interest in books were teased 'for putting on airs . . . the "smart one" who thinks he is not "one of us"' (Berube 1996: 146). He suggests that those who transcend their class background through education are faced with 'unresolved conflicts about what you have lost and gained . . . [and] the anguish of leaving a home you can't return to while not belonging where you've ended up' (Ibid.: 140).

Narratives such as that of Berube have traditionally been less prominent than the dominant **redemption narrative** that is part of a wider discourse, a discourse in which education is positioned as the antidote to class inequality. The role of making explicit alternative stories, those narratives that are less visible or known, is seen as another of the strengths of narrative inquiry, as it can lead to social change by inserting less well-known narratives that oppose or disrupt dominant cultural discourses. However, in the case of academics from lower socio-economic backgrounds, Berube is not convinced. In his view, articulating 'a class escape story' within middle-class university settings

> only reinforces class hierarchies in the telling. Even as it makes visible and validates the lives of working-class people, and evokes sympathy from middle-class listeners, it reduces us to either victims or heroes. Our lives become satisfying dramas of suffering that end in inspiring victory or poignant tragedy.
>
> (Berube 1996: 154)

STORIES AS RESISTANCE

The issue of balancing the possibility of bringing about change through making alternative narratives explicit while guarding against the possibility that such narratives will get subordinated or assimilated into the dominant narrative is a serious one in research. There is no answer that brings with it the surety of right or wrong: it is a matter of judgement on the part of the researcher and requires deep consideration of the ethics involved in narrative research practice.

Rather than thinking about a second version of the extract in which the discomfort of the atypical academic is reinforced, the life-writer might have storied a much more resistant version. A resistant story might take the position that university education strongly encourages types of thinking and behaviour different from that valued in lower socio-economic class groups. Educational institutions encouraging and insisting on particular kinds of behaviour may be seen as fitting with more radical, but much less visible, narratives about the true nature of education. A resistant view could see education as an instrument of the State, and its aims – rather than encouraging the free and full expression of ideas by those who attend – as actually to discipline bodies and produce docile and normative citizens. Citizens who are disciplined in such ways are more likely to conform to shared ideals of civility, and are thus more predictable and hence more control-able by the establishment and the State.

However, this type of **resistance narrative** would challenge the writer's continued professional status as an academic. At the very least, it would invoke some dissonance with a professional identity that invests heavily in the positive effects of education: it would be difficult to see how he could remain within an institution that he viewed as subordinating the values and ideals of the socio-economic class group in which he was raised.

Resistance narratives, of the kind previously explored in terms of university education, can often be seen in the literary works of writers who want to disrupt, and therefore change, the widely accepted and taken-for-granted narratives in our culture. Literary writers who explicitly explore themes of cultural politics are likely to adopt a form of resistance narrative in their writing. Angela Carter's re-telling of classic fairytales, for example in *The Bloody Chamber* (1995), exemplifies this approach when she attempts to disrupt cultural understandings of femininity by radically changing the role of the female protagonist in the classic tale.

While Carter's focus was on gender, the work of Jean Rhys (1890–1979) focused on race in her novel *Wide Sargasso Sea* (2000 [1966]). Her novel is a postcolonial 'prequel' to Charlotte Brontë's *Jane Eyre*. Rhys, who was born in Dominica, gives the narrative voice in her novel to a figure assumed to be Bertha, Mr Rochester's wife, who appears in *Jane Eyre* as a 'madwoman in the attic'. Rhys details how Bertha's life in the Caribbean, her inter-racial marriage to Rochester and her relocation to the patriarchal culture and harsh climate of England cause her mental breakdown.

In *Longbourn* (2014), Jo Baker re-tells the story of Jane Austen's *Pride and Prejudice* from the perspective of the servants, enabling her to focus on social class and represent the daily chores of the household rather than the peccadillos of the ruling classes. For example, the nar-rator represents the thoughts of Sarah, one of the servants: 'If Elizabeth Bennet had the washing of her own petticoats, Sarah thought, she would be more careful not to trudge through muddy fields'.

Poetry also has its share of resistance narration – narrative as a form does not have to be fashioned as prose fiction. For example, in her poetry collection *The World's Wife* (2010), the current Poet

Laureate, Carol Ann Duffy, gives voice to the following characters: Anne Hathaway (Shakespeare's wife), Queen Kong, Delilah, Frau Freud, Mrs Quasimodo and the Kray sisters.

Resistance narratives can also be seen in artistic forms beyond literary works. There are many examples of resistance in music and fine art, for example. Political protest can be articulated in an engaging way, in which messages are all the more powerful for their satirical stance. The YouTube link below is an example of this. It features the rap group Boom Chicago, satirising the infamous 'Zwarte Piet' tradition in the Netherlands, where 'Sinterklaas' (the Father Christmas figure) is said to arrive on 5 December with his 'little black helper' who performs menial tasks. Watch the rap and decide how this approach might compare with a more conventional anti-racist protest or critique: www.youtube.com/watch?v=vyTW-S0yTiI.

You could also explore the work of the Adbusters organisation (search for 'Adbusters' online) which, as its name suggests, creates advertising messages that overturn the many slogans and watchwords embedded in contemporary culture by commercial companies. Sally Swain's *Great Housewives of Art* books (1988) offer a visual equivalent of Carol Ann Duffy's poetry by taking a wry look at the 'great masters' from the perspective of their wives.

Resistance narratives can also be identified in talk about everyday aspects of life. For example, Fisher and Freshwater (2014) demonstrate the value of narrative inquiry in listening to the stories of mental illness by those who experience it rather than to those who diagnose and treat it. In so doing, new templates for understanding mental illness can emerge, thus facilitating 'alternatives for imagining and living with mental illness' (2014: 204). They argue that people living with mental illness have disrupted, or even refused, the role of passive patient assigned to them in the dominant view promoted by the medical profession. By this means, people living with mental illness have attempted to change the ways they are treated and how they therefore experience their mental health. Arthur Frank (1995) has written extensively and more generally about illness from a narrative point of view.

There are many further resistance narratives that can be explored and many more that can be imagined. A starting point for thinking further about this area could be to stand back and identify some more examples of powerful mainstream cultural narratives, those that are so often repeated that they pass under our critical radar – for example, 'rags to riches' stories or 'happy ever after' romances. Then it is possible to think about creative disruptions and acts of resistance.

9

DISCOURSE AND IDENTITY

AIMS OF THIS CHAPTER

This chapter will:

- explore the meaning of the term 'identity' and explain how academic views of this concept have changed; and
- contextualise the changes in thinking about identity, and link them with some specific philosophical traditions.

EVERYDAY MEANINGS OF 'IDENTITY'

A search of the British National Corpus (BNC) offers 100 random examples of the word 'identity' in different contexts. Here are some frequently repeated usages:

identity card	identity theft	identity parade
proof of identity	mistaken identity	true identity
hidden identity	a sense of identity	losing your identity
European identity	national identity	local identity
regional identity	working class identity	personal identity
identity crisis	cultural identity	corporate identity

You might be able to add some examples of your own from popular media, or from your own experience.

The BNC examples illustrate some ways of thinking about identity that are embedded in contemporary society and institutional practices. They suggest that identity is a thing that people possess – it can be shown and proved; it can be lost, stolen or hidden. Identity can be 'true' or 'false', and one identity can be mistaken for another. This conceptualises identity as a set of facts that can verify (identify) who someone is.

The BNC examples also show that identity is seen as existing in different forms, not so much as a set of facts, but more as qualities and categories we might associate ourselves with ('identify with'): locality and region, social class, the State, a continent, a culture. It is seen as something that can pertain to individuals ('personal') but also something that organisations can acquire ('corporate').

Unsurprisingly, dictionary definitions bear out the descriptions above. The Cambridge Dictionary defines 'identity' as 'who a person is, or the qualities of a person or group that make them different from others'. The Oxford Dictionary definition differentiates between 'facts' and 'characteristics' of identity: 'the fact of being who or what a person or thing is'; 'the characteristics determining who or what a person or thing is'.

ACADEMIC DEFINITIONS

Academic approaches to identity show some commonality with the everyday meanings. Some researchers are interested in the whole question of identity cards, State surveillance and individual rights to privacy, and, to that extent, their focus is on how identity 'facts' are expressed, owned, managed and put to use. Others focus more on the idea of categories and characteristics, looking at how and why people have attachments to the rather more abstract notions of class, culture, region and nation.

A distinctive difference between discourse approaches to identity and that of everyday meanings (and also some other academic areas) is that identity is not seen as an unchanging 'reality'. The dictionary definitions above both use the verb 'to be': 'who a person or thing *is*'. From a discourse perspective, identity is something that is fluid, continually being constructed and how a person or thing *seems*.

A further difference is that identities are seen as performed by choices of language and other symbolic resources, rather than language being the result of an identity that was already there. This means that we are what we perform, rather than performing what we are: identity is a product, a creation. This idea can be teased out a little by referring to the work of Erving Goffman whose work was quoted in Chapter 7.

Goffman (1969) used a dramaturgical metaphor for social life, seeing identity as a set of performances and members of society as performing in much the same way as actors in a play. Like actors, we learn a 'script' for situations but the best performances are customised and seemingly spontaneous. If we carry out a similar performance enough times in the same contexts, we acquire an identity, a sense of self as a stable entity, and others see us in this light. Different contexts require us to give different performances, so we need to be able to play different roles. If you want to explore that idea in your own life, you could think about the different kinds of performances you give in the different aspects of your life – for example, student, parent, child, employer, employee, sports fan or player – and describe how your performances in these roles vary. For example, does your language change? Does your code of dress change? How about your non-verbal behaviour? And how do others' attitudes to you change when you are inhabiting these different identities?

STUDIES OF LANGUAGE AND IDENTITY

There is a substantial history within sociolinguistics dating from the 1960s of studying the relationship between language and social group identities such as region, social class, gender and ethnicity. Chapter 3 referred to early studies of language and gender, where some sociolinguists claimed that many meanings in the English language privileged a male view of the world, and that women were socialised into ways of speaking that were then dismissed as 'powerless'. Since that early point, work on how men and women are represented in discourses has continued to point up differential treatment of the sexes, so the picture is one of continuity of research approach. And in the area of representation, some changes have occurred in real-world usage. For example, writers of all kinds are much more aware nowadays of the problems of sex-typed job titles and the fact that English has no neutral **generic pronoun**. So titles such as 'policeman' and 'air stewardess' have changed to 'police officer' and 'cabin crew'; and the use of 'he' supposedly to refer to both sexes has largely disappeared. (Early studies of the use of 'he' for supposed inclusive reference showed its use in some comically inappropriate texts such as advice on physically giving birth, which demonstrated how uninclusive the use of 'he' actually was.) This area of language change and the whole question of the relationship between language and the world it represents – an area first discussed in Chapter 3 of this book – is often part of public debates about so-called 'political correctness' (PC) (or 'language reform', to describe it more positively). Arguments about representation and language change obviously extend way beyond the area of gender and encompass all the aspects of social identity referred to at the beginning of this section, and more – for example, age, disability, sexuality, religious affiliation, occupation.

Arguments about so-called PC often revolve around the way language is used for labelling different groups. That is clearly an issue, but linguistic representation is much more subtle and deep-rooted than this. As Chapters 3 and 4 showed, language items are not simply surface features that are stuck onto a referent; instead they involve a complex network of implicit meanings that are built up over time and passed on through generations of language users. Chapter 3 referred to the way in which romantic fiction often positions male and female figures as active and passive, respectively; but there are many further types of text that build representations more subtly, using our experience of how language has been used before in all the texts we have encountered. For example, look at the commonly used verbs below and think about the type of figure you would normally imagine as the person doing the action – is that figure normally male or female? Does changing the sex of the subject disrupt the image you would normally have when the word is used?:

[X] *flounced* out of the room   [X] *strode* across the room
[X] *shrieked with joy*   [X] was *gossiping* and *giggling* in the corner

So far, the discussion has been about representation, but sociolinguists are perhaps better known for studying the language of speakers themselves – a focus on language users, rather than language use. In terms of researching the language used by male and female speakers, a great deal has changed. The changes include a recognition that to have such all-encompassing categories as 'men' and 'women' is unworkable; that research on male and female speakers in the USA could not and should not be generalised to other cultures; and that even within one culture, there are significant large-scale factors such as age and ethnicity that interconnect with gender, as well as a whole range of situational factors such as setting and audience. For example, Tannen (1981) explored the relationship between gender and cultural background in several studies, showing how language features that had been seen rather simplistically in early research as markers of dominance or subordination in conversations, and associated with one sex or the other, can be seen as much more complex phenomena when the cultural background of the participants is factored in. There are many accessible collections of research on language and gender and some of these can be found in the further reading lists at the back of this book.

Other areas of sociolinguistics focus on language and culture more broadly, and this was the case in the work of John Gumperz, who was referred to in Chapter 7. Gumperz has worked particularly on language and social inequality and on intercultural communication. His focus on inference and implicit meanings pointed up how inequality can result from a lack of transparency by those in more powerful positions about their own meanings; and an inability by those with less power to access mainstream hidden meanings and assumptions. As a typical example, a research paper by Akinnato and Ajirotutu from an early collection edited by Gumperz (1983) illustrates some interview data where an applicant from an ethnic minority is applying for a job in a library. The interviewer then asks the following question, and the interview proceeds as outlined below:

Interviewer:	what about the library interests you most?
Applicant:	what about the library in terms of the books? (1.0) or the whole building?

Interviewer:	any point that you'd like to make
Applicant:	oh, the children's books (.) because I have a child (.) and the children (1.0) you know (.) there's so many (.) you know (.) books for them to read (.) you know (.) and little things that would interest them (.) would interest me too

When the interviewer says 'any point you'd like to make', this isn't really giving the interviewee carte blanche to refer to any aspect of the library. For example, you wouldn't expect an applicant to talk about the paintwork or the cleaning bill; this is an applicant being given the chance to showcase their thinking. The applicant does pick up on the word 'interest' and recognises that this is an opportunity to register some professional expertise, but in identifying with children the impression given is one of immaturity. You might be able to recall some similar examples, particularly in interview situations, where you had to recognise the real, hidden question behind the question that was ostensibly being asked.

The interview example above focused on the pragmatics of inter-ethnic communication. Other sociolinguistic studies have focused on inequality and regional identities, particularly with reference to the position of non-standard English users and the social power and status attributed to certain varieties of English. Examples of regional English have been collected for many years by **dialectologists**, and it is clear that there are distinctive differences between the grammatical structures of regional dialects and those of **standard English**, which is the nearest that English has to an official written language (standard English is a concept that linguists attach more to writing than to speech). **Regional dialect vocabulary** has been dying out over the years, along with older working practices and ways of living in isolated communities. However, regionally based grammatical structures are still extant. One of the most obvious differences between regional dialects and standard English is the verb 'to be'; standard English in the past tense uses a mixture of 'was' and 'were' in the singular:

Singular (i.e. reference to one person)	Plural (i.e. reference to more than one person)
I *was*	We *were*
You *were*	You *were*
He, she, it, one *was*	They *were*

Some regional dialects use 'was' throughout the system – for example, older speakers of London Cockney dialect may do this, while other dialects will use 'were' throughout – for example, some dialects in the north-west region of England.

The basis for labelling certain forms as 'regional dialect' rather than 'errors' of usage is that large numbers of people in a particular region will use those forms frequently and consistently (see Milroy and Milroy 1993), and the features involved can include verb tenses, prepositions, pronouns and other commonly used items. **Regional dialect grammar** often demonstrates regularity so, as exemplified by the dialect forms of the verb 'to be', there will often be one form that is used throughout. There is an argument therefore that regional dialects can be seen as more efficient – and, because of their regularity, easier to learn. However, in public discourses about 'correctness', regional dialect grammar is often stigmatised as signalling speaker ignorance and lack of education. A language feature can be used as a **shibboleth** – a linguistic 'marker' or test word, determining whether an individual is allowed entry to a social group, showing whether the applicant comes with the right badge of identity – whether he or she 'speaks the right language'.

Historically, standard English was itself a form of regional language but it emerged as a favoured variety as a result of the commercial growth and prosperity of the London area. Standard English is nothing to do with high standards, and it includes both formal and informal styles of English, so it is inclusive of slang (see Trudgill 1999 for a useful list of what standard English *isn't*). However, it is this variety that has been **codified**, forming the basis for norms of usage that are taught in schools and to learners of English as an additional language. It is therefore often seen as *the* English language, when in fact there are many other varieties that are equally valid.

Crowley (1989), Milroy and Milroy (1998) and Aitchison (2001) are among many linguists who have explored public attitudes to

tandard and non-standard varieties of English in a field that could be
ermed, after the title of Crowley's book, 'the politics of discourse'.
Aitchison identifies a phenomenon she terms **declinism**, showing
hat those who want to keep the status quo often look back to a
golden age' when language use was supposedly perfect – except that
everyone pegs this at a different point. Metaphors of rot and decay
and images of crumbling castles and civilisation under threat abound
n public debates about how language has gone to the dogs, and the
culprits are the usual suspects – young people, the mass media, pop
music (especially rap), the working classes.

Milroy and Milroy talk of an ongoing **complaint tradition**, seeing this as a specific powerplay by people, typically those from a
privileged background, about the supposedly poor language use of
those who are often working-class, regional speakers. Crowley sees
this strategy as a way for those in power to deflect others' claims
and maintain their own positions. The complaint of 'it's not what
you say, it's the way that you say it' diverts attention from substan-
tive issues to focus on aspects of style and language choice. The real
point at issue is actually not language at all, but the fears of people
in establishment positions that their power may be eroded if others'
claims are acceded to. Saying that it's impossible to understand the
language of others, claiming that it lacks clarity and is confused, that
ideas are not being expressed properly – these complaints are part of
a power game that goes way beyond language itself.

Debates about standard English extend beyond the UK to encompass questions about the nature of international English and the
identities of its speakers. Historically, international norms of English
centred on what Kachru (1990) has called 'the inner circle' of countries such as the UK, the USA and Australia – anglophone countries
with large numbers of native speakers. More recently, distinct varieties
of English have evolved in many postcolonial communities in areas
such as the Caribbean, South East Asia, India and West Africa. These
are termed variously as **New Englishes** or World Englishes. And
more recently still, the spread of English has accelerated as a result of
globalisation to reach countries where English has only ever existed as
a foreign language – for example, across eastern Europe and in Japan.

Because so many different communities now have a stake in
English, linguists working in the area of international English have

questioned the assumptions made in many texts – for example teaching materials – that norms of usage should be based on native speakers. Saraceni (2010) talks of the need to 'relocate' English maintaining at the very least that materials for learners of English should stop picturing the characteristic red postboxes and other iconic images of 'old England'; and also calling for a halt to the idea that 'inner circle' countries somehow own English and can therefore arbitrate on usage.

Another reason for arguing for relocation is that, with digital communication systems, English users anywhere in the world can be online with each other. In other words, language use isn't connected with a physically based identity in the way it once was. Constantly referring back to a time when it was constrained in this way therefore makes even less sense.

As a small example of what this may mean in practice, look at the exchange below. This is from a conversation between two students who were working online together on an international project. Dave is in the UK and Helene is in Sweden. Dave is a monolingual speaker of English and Helene is bilingual in Swedish and English. Their online conversations are conducted in English, so this is an example of **English as a lingua franca** – English used in a context where at least one participant is not a native speaker. Dave attempts to correct Helene on her spelling of a word, and it happens to be one where there is no agreed format because it is normally part of informal speech and is not written down very often. The exchange shows that in a globalised world, native speaker norms are open to contestation – in Helene's case, a challenge carried out with humour and good grace:

Dave>>	by the way, It might be best to say 'okay' rather than okey
Helene>>	okey!
Dave>>	sorry and all that!!!
Helene>>	okey! :)

(Goddard 2011)

CHANGING IDEAS ABOUT IDENTITY AND NOTIONS OF SELF

The following sentence occurred in the previous section: 'A further difference is that identities are seen as performed by choices of language and other symbolic resources, rather than language being the result of an identity that was already there'. This was used in the context of explaining how sociolinguistic scholarship has changed over time, in its attitude to identity. The section below takes further the idea of changing definitions of identity and introduces some areas of critical thinking that have been influential, particularly in the Social Sciences.

Questions of 'who am I' and the relationships between that 'I' and wider social structures have been central to academic scholarship, especially in disciplines like Psychology, Sociology and Human Geography. It would be impossible to recount the development of these academic ideas within each of these disciplines in a short chapter, but one of the frameworks devised by Stuart Hall can help to demonstrate the shift in thinking towards the idea of the 'I' which is a product, an effect, of performance. Although Hall is most closely associated with Cultural Studies – indeed, he is considered the founder of modern Cultural Studies in the UK – his work has had a significant impact in shaping identity scholarship in the Social Sciences, including its development over time.

Hall's (1996) much-published chapter *The Question of Cultural Identity* characterises three distinct conceptions of identity that have emerged across the Social Sciences (and to some degree in the Humanities) over time. The three strands proposed by Hall are:

- the enlightenment subject;
- the sociological subject; and
- the postmodern subject.

Note here that 'subject' is neither a grammatical category nor a 'topic': it is used here to mean an 'identity'.

Before continuing, it is important to note that Hall's framework is not a theory of identity per se. Rather, he provides a broad characterisation of identity theories as developed in other disciplines. A further point to recognise is that although the three strands of thinking developed consecutively over time, the development of one did not erase the other: proponents of each of the traditions continue to hold sway to different degrees and in different disciplines. You may well be more familiar with one conception of identity than another, depending on the discipline or area of academic study in which you are located.

THE ENLIGHTENMENT SUBJECT

This name derives from the conception of subjectivity in the intellectual traditions associated with an era of time called the **Enlightenment**, the origins of which are variously ascribed to the seventeenth or eighteenth centuries. The period is characterised by a rejection of traditional values, including religion and superstition, with a move towards valuing knowledge that relied on reason and rationality. Ideas that developed from scientific progress were seen as especially important. The Enlightenment, closely associated with a broad philosophical tradition known as **humanism** (Davies 1997), is seen as the period when our modern ideas of the individual emerged and were subsequently consolidated through a range of academic and political belief systems. The concept of the enlightenment 'subject' is one of identity as core attributes – a set of characteristics possessed by an individual, making up the inner essence of their 'selfhood'. Identity consists of traits that mark our uniqueness, engineers our experience of the world, and is more or less fixed and static across the lifespan. According to this broad view, on the basis of some sort of **essence** – and there has never been agreement about what the basis of that essence might be – the rational thinking individual is seen as fully in control of their consciousness and actions.

This view of identity has characterised many traditions within Psychology, with efforts to identify and explain differences across individuals on the basis of psychological structures like personality traits and levels of innate intelligence. It is a view of identity that is also evident in biological and medical discourses that locate he essence of one's being in biological structures – most recently ocated in genes and in brain or other neurological mechanisms. This **biological determinism** can also be seen in theories of sexual and gender identity that explain differences between men and women or between straight and gay as a function of 'natural' biological differences.

Hall suggests that this conception of the 'self' is one that s firmly embedded in the mundane language of popular culture. Such language highlights 'natural' talents or abilities in accounting for differences in achievements or social position as opposed to focusing on the social and cultural conditions that may account for these differences. For example, in education environments, language labels of various kinds fix identities in categories such as 'gifted' or 'slow', and whole groups of people might be constructed as lazy and feckless (working-class or racial groups), over-emotional (women and homosexuals), or having 'natural' physical abilities (black people). In these language constructions, it is the role of nature rather than nurture that is credited as the significant feature of identity.

The idea that identity is a function of biology is one that has been played out recently in controversies about athletes and gender surrounding the South African athlete Caster Semenya. Semenya's status as a female runner has been called into question and has been subjected to a range of medical examinations which show that she does not have a womb or ovaries and has levels of testosterone that are more characteristic of men. The controversy surrounding Semenya's participation in world athletics is, of course, of specific concern for the athlete and her ability to compete and build a career as a successful middle-distance runner. But the controversy also has wider relevance in relation to understandings about the nature of masculinity and femininity more generally. As an exercise, you could follow the newspaper debates surrounding Semenya's career, exploring how these debates implicate wider discourses related to gender and sexuality. Here is an example from the *i*, a UK-based newspaper. The article shows some of the complexities around basing definitions of gender identity on ideas of 'naturalness' and biological norms:

Semenya's dominance fuels debate over her eligibility

Caster Semenya is going nowhere, and neither is the sizeable problem she presents and represents. On Saturday, Semenya won the 400, the 800, and 1,500 metres at the South African Senior Athletics Championships. It was history-making. Semenya, of course, was temporarily suspended in 2009, until she took provisions to lower her naturally high levels of testosterone. In the summer of 2015, the Court of Arbitration for Sport wiped out those regulations. Semenya can run at her 'normal' levels again – and the debate over whether that's right will rage on.

(Cutler 2016)

The idea of the enlightenment subject goes beyond representations of particular individuals in the public eye. It also features in everyday language use, in expressions that index a true, if hidden, self waiting to be revealed. Phrases such as 'I'm not myself today' or 'I'd like you to know the real me' are two examples in a much wider lexicon of mundane speech that indexes an authentic inner core of identity. Benwell and Stokoe (2006) talk of the idea of identity as 'a project of the self' and show how this is exemplified in self-help literature and mainstream print and television media where you are encouraged to be your best self or where a target individual – a proxy for you – is exhorted to change current behaviours that do not reflect the 'real' person underneath. Below are some examples from popular self-help literature on ageing – there are many more titles like these. A theme running through not just their titles but their respective 'blurbs' is that scientific advancements will enable the 'real you' to be revealed:

Reverse the Signs of Ageing
The Anti-Ageing Manual
The Science of Ageing Backward: Re-Generation-X
The Age Fix

HE SOCIOLOGICAL SUBJECT

'or Hall, the conception of the sociological subject shifted the focus rom identity as characteristics fixed in the individual towards a focus n how identity is formed through relations with others, with the ocial. According to this view our sense of 'who am I?' is shaped n and through our interactions with others. From an early age it s close significant others – parents, carers, family – that inform our ense of who we are and how we fit into the world. As we grow lder, our identity – or more properly, identities – is shaped in and y interactions with wider institutions like school, peer and social roupings, workplaces, as well as the mass media and legal frame- works that operate in the societies within which we are located. These processes of identity formation involve establishing our ameness to, and difference from, our sense of those others with whom we engage daily either in social interaction or through media representations.

An example of a sociological approach to identity can be seen in studies of how participants in interactions create their identities discursively. For example, in the study of mascu- line identities by Edley and Wetherell (1997) titled 'Jockeying for position: the construction of masculine identities', sixth-form boys in a single-sex school talked about the perceived status of attributes associated with different masculine identities, such as the idea of being a 'new man' and what that entailed. Similarly, Coates (2003) demonstrates how ideas about masculinity are produced discursively (and, in particular, narratively) in adult male talk in relaxed social situations. She focuses specifically on casual conversation because she sees this site as key in identity formation and maintenance: 'Identity work . . . is one of the key functions of talk among friends. In talk with close friends, we can explore who we are in a more relaxed way than in other, more formal, contexts' (Coates 2003: 2).

As well as creating and maintaining identities when talking to people we know, we are also identifying with and against more abstract and imagined others with whom we may not have imme- diate interaction – like the 'criminal', the 'foreigner', the 'insane'. We also locate our sense of self in relation to complex and abstract ideas about, and ideals of, being: of being good, of being happy, of being beautiful, of being healthy, of being masculine or feminine, of being young or old, of being straight or gay. In this way we identify with and adopt individual and group identities whose significance is invested in social labels that are shared within cultures. Most importantly, we negotiate this socially constructed sense of self in relation to cultural norms of such categories of being. Thus, our sense of self is regulated not just in our own processes of identification, but in the rich cultural and linguistic landscapes with which we engage in everyday talk and text, including the social categories of identity referred to above.

Many of the theories that align with this view of identity reject conceptions of identity, or any features associated with it, that locate it in innate characteristics of the individual. Instead, social and cultural surroundings are highlighted as key resources in the development of identity. In effect, the emphasis in these theories is on the role of nurture over that of nature in the formation of identity. The sociological view aligns with common-sense notions about how we become socialised as fully functioning members of the society to which we belong. According to such theoretical conceptions of identity, at the heart of these processes of identification remains the idea of a core of self that is, in effect, in charge of moderating its interactions and negotiations with the social and cultural world. Unlike the enlightenment subject outlined, which locates the individual's identity in some innate and naturally occurring (often biologically based) phenomenon, the 'core' of the sociological subject is most usually configured as some form of inner consciousness that is knowingly and reflexively interacting with the outer social world. It is through this 'knowing interactivity' that the 'self' learns and maintains its best fit in the wider social milieu.

To get a tangible sense of how these processes of socialisation happen in textual form, you could choose a magazine that is targeted at an audience segment that aligns with how you currently identify. Read through the magazine and think about how the target audience is constructed by reflecting on the magazine's title, the various features included, the use of images and the particular uses of language.

HE POSTMODERN SUBJECT

According to Hall's framework, the postmodern subject is conceived in radically different ways than in the previous two conceptions of subjectivity or identity. According to such theoretical approaches, identity is not located *in* the individual, nor is it negotiated *by* a core consciousness of the individual, but rather it functions *on* the body as a product of a range of discourses available in the culture in which individuals – as social bodies – are located.

These views of identity often highlight the plasticity and fluidity of identity and celebrate the kinds of creative freedoms available for individuals and groups to fashion new, multiple and sometimes resistant identifications. However, such views also underscore the anxieties and crises attendant on the possibility that identities are fully malleable, seeing identity formations as open to manipulation through those discourses that serve the agendas of powerful interests like governments and multinational companies promoting their particular brands. In contrast to both the enlightenment and sociological views outlined, with postmodernism there is greater scepticism about the role of individual agency in exercising control over identity formation within the chaotic flux of social changes that are represented through multiple and competing discourses. Instead, individual agency is considered, at best, fragmented and contradictory in its ability to author itself and to regulate the effects of cultural discourses in the production of identities.

According to these views, the very notions of 'self', 'individual' or 'identity' are a product of language and discourse. It is via language and discourse that the categories of identity exist and through which a sense of self takes on meaning. For example, what it means to identify as a man or woman, young or old, straight or gay is dependent on the multiple discourses available in culture for these subject positions. As a reminder here, it is important to note that the discourses that shape possibilities for identity refer to more than just language: other cultural practices like play, fashion, food, music and leisure activities are implicated in forming identity by prescribing and proscribing certain norms and forms of behaviour.

This postmodern conception of identity reflects a range of academic disciplines' attempts to re-think identity in the face of dramatic socio-political changes occurring in the latter decades of the twentieth century and continuing into the present – an er referred to as **postmodernity**. Some of the changes associate with this period include the growth of new technologies, the rise o **hyper-capitalism** following the demise of European **socialism** and a radical critique of those socio-political values that attached t ideas of progress and rationality. Another significant feature of thi period is the emergence of increasingly strident political movement seeking visibility and equality for those traditionally marginalise from mainstream society. In addition, there were, and still are, call to recognise how even formerly marginalised identities (women blacks, gays and lesbians) are shaped in multiple and contradictory ways in contemporary society, meaning that identifications migh be fleeting, can change rapidly and are contingent on the contex within which people are located. Cultural industries and glo-balised mass media are seen as instrumental in furnishing a range o new identity models to which audiences might align their sense o identity.

These approaches – mainly developed in Cultural Studies – are interested in the ways in which cultural discourses facilitate and constrain different identity positions that are, in turn, enacted and performed in everyday life. Rather than focusing exclusively on how individuals negotiate and ascribe their own and others' identity as a function of some kind of inner core that has the final say, more atten-tion is paid to the cultural discourses that render identity positions available and allow bodies to perform a continual 'becoming' into ever-changing identity positions. As Benwell and Stokoe (2006: 4) maintain, 'Who we are to each other, then, is accomplished, disputed, ascribed, resisted, managed and negotiated in discourse'.

DISCOURSES ABOUT AGE AND IDENTITY

The three broad ways of conceiving of identity outlined in the last few pages are, most likely, not delineated neatly and packaged up conveniently in talk and text. Instead, what can face a discourse analyst is a complex network of discourses that are in play and that offer contradictory ideas within even a small sample of data. Consider the topic of age and ageing, which is a dimension not yet fully considered in this book.

Earlier in this chapter there were some examples of self-help books that appeared to suggest an enlightenment idea of age. This same concept can also be seen in the many legal frameworks that delineate the specific ages at which we can engage in a broad range of activities like leaving school, driving, voting, having sex, getting married, retiring from work or drawing a pension. Legally sanctioned age distinctions are fundamentally based on enlightenment ideas of identity that frame the ability to do something along a linear trajectory of age.

However, there are also more nebulous cultural frames that sanction age-appropriate behaviour. Contemporary Western societies are often characterised as youth-obsessed, rendering older people as undervalued, redundant or even a burden for such societies.

Chapter 4 explored a semiotic approach to discourse and noted how discourses structure both our sense of reality and our notion of our own identity. Contemporary UK road signs articulate a negative view of ageing, with elderly, frail figures bent-backed with life's cares and dependent on walking sticks (and with the woman walking behind the man, as if for support). There are also many negative metaphors for ageing, including orientation metaphors like 'being over the hill' and 'at the end of the road'. Growing old in Western societies is often symbolised in the **metonym** of grey hair and is associated with no longer being productive. The idea of growing old is often constructed as similar to that of being a child, or not being fully an adult, and this construction is even more ingrained as the conception of adulthood is more and more closely entwined with the idea of being a productive citizen of the economically oriented nation state.

Old age as a topic in the media is often discussed with reference to the social care necessary to deal with an ageing population. In the context of such discussions, dementia and other chronic health conditions associated with ageing are often couched in catastrophic terms, as a tsunami or a fate worse than death (Peel 2014), or through metaphors of war, signifying the seriousness and unpredictability of the societal issues that are being faced, including the significant costs associated with people living longer.

In contrast to the dystopian picture outlined above is the idea of the 'young-old' – an apparent **oxymoron** but expressing the conceptualisation of old age as retaining the characteristics of younger age groups such as the middle-aged. This new young-old identity comprises a whole slew of other terms and prescriptions: health ageing, successful ageing, active ageing – a new kind of ageing, where older people are invoked to stay engaged socially, physically and cognitively to ensure better physical and mental health at later stages of life (see Moulaert and Biggs 2016). These discourses prescribe how best to do it – look younger, stay active, keep healthy. You can see these ideas expressed in the book titles below, which are further examples from the self-help bookshelves:

> *Ageing, Health and Productivity*
> *Feel Fabulous Forever*
> *Sod Seventy!*
> *Grow Younger, Live Longer*
> *Living the Life Unexpected: 12 Weeks to Your Plan B for a Meaningful and Fulfilling Future Without Children*

Some argue that these conceptions of new ageing are neo-liberal in kind – insinuating a moral responsibility on the individual to maintain their health so that they do not become a burden.

But there are inevitable further discourses around this 'new-old' identity. The idea of the 'sexy oldie' (Gott 2005) is at odds not only with older stereotypes of 'asexual old age' but also with that of 'growing old gracefully' and not appearing as 'mutton dressed as lamb'.

It is the work of discourse analysts to tease out such different discourses and to be aware of the **intersectional** nature of all identities – in this case, age, sexuality and gender.

10

COLLECTING AND REPRESENTING DISCOURSE

AIMS OF THIS CHAPTER

If discourse is about doing something – performing a role, expressing an identity, acting out a script, constructing a reality, creating meanings – then it would be odd to come to the end of a book on discourse without thinking about doing something with discourse as a researcher. If you have read the rest of this book, then hopefully by now you have a good understanding of the nature of discourse, and of the many academic fields and approaches that are possible in researching it.

This chapter assumes that you want to go further, and think about how to make a start in collecting some discourse to answer a research question. You may need to do this at some future point, in which case this chapter will act as a form of preparation for that work. You may have been asked to critique some research that has already been done, in which case you could read this chapter with a focus on how that researcher went about their task. Or you may be specifically interested in the logistic, political or even philosophical questions that researching discourse can pose. In that case, this chapter will inform your thinking and help to shape your subsequent actions. The chapter begins by covering some of the practical skills that researchers in all fields – not just discourse analysts – need to acquire.

GENERAL RESEARCH SKILLS

Research skills take time to acquire. However, because they can b
broken down into specific sub-skills, they can be considered on
by one, and it may be the case that you are already expert in som
of these while still developing others. You could therefore treat thi
section as a kind of checklist in auditing your progress on the researc
skills trajectory. The section is not just about skills in researching th
topic of discourse, so you could use it for any research you are doing
however, researching discourse does require all the skills outlined i
this section to be in play.

PLANNING AND DEADLINES

It is important to break any task down into stages. Not only doe
this help you to see what has to be done, but also it is psychologi-
cally reassuring to see that there are steps and resting points along the
way – you don't have to scale the mountain in one leap. Breaking
down a whole activity into stages is something that is not just
done in academic work – it is a familiar process in everyday activities such as following a recipe or constructing a piece of flat-pack
furniture. However, as you will know from your experiences of the
latter activities, sometimes things do not go to plan and you take
much longer than the time you originally set aside.

When you are planning, work backwards from any deadline and
peg each stage to a date. Then go through the schedule again and
think more carefully about which stages will be more demanding
than others, and add extra time for those. Although deadlines might
need to be seen as a little elastic, there needs to be a cut-off point
where, if things have not been achieved, you might need to change
tack, abandon your original idea and adopt an alternative path.

Having read the other chapters in this book, you are of course
noticing the flurry of metaphors used above to describe academic
work – mountain climbing, sailing (tacking), hiking (path), home
craft (pegs and elastic), warfare and print journalism (deadline,
the original meaning of which was a line that soldiers imprisoned
in stockades in the American Civil War were not allowed to cross,
on pain of being shot). It isn't surprising that research work should

e described as a physical enterprise, because there are physical tasks nd constraints associated with it; and it is also understandable that cademic inquiry is seen as a journey, with challenges involved en oute and rewards at the end (the view from the mountaintop, get-ng wind in the sails and the exhilaration of speed).

However, two important things are obscured in using these netaphors. One is that good research is often very small-scale, vhich doesn't match with the idea of scaling mountains or crossing oceans in record time. Researchers who struggle are often those vho are over-ambitious in their plans, with aims that are unreal-stic and therefore unachievable. So the 'big adventure' idea needs o be tempered by the perception that 'small is beautiful': a care-ully conducted small-scale plan which is realistic and achievable s likely to be much more successful – and therefore a much more ewarding adventure – than a grand plan that has little chance of ctually being realised.

The second reason why physical adventure metaphors do not capture the research (or learning) process well is that they do not highlight the activity of thinking, which is a fundamental part of research work. Thinking is of course physical but it is not framed eas-ily as a discrete activity that only happens at point a or b. Researchers typically spend as much or even more time thinking about their data than collecting it, but in making a schedule people don't often mark days as 'thinking' time. In fact, thinking happens alongside, around, before, after and during data collection, and probably also a long time after the project is finished. Thinking – weighing up ideas, questioning and critiquing existing research or assumed concepts, wondering if x or y could be the case – is what research is all about.

Making a plan and managing deadlines are not only a part of academic inquiry; they are also key skills in the workplace and in life more generally. You could therefore think about how to credit yourself on your CV for the different skills that you develop as you conduct any piece of research.

HAVING A PLAN B

In the previous sub-section some advice was given about abandon-ing a plan if, by a certain point, no progress had been made. It was suggested that researchers need a 'Plan B', which can act as a safety net (research as high-wire acrobatics). A Plan B can come in many different forms. It could involve continuing to use the existing plan for data collection, but changing the aims and focus of the research question. It could involve changing or recalculating the range of data sources being used: for example, an individual or group may have promised to submit some data to you but nothing has been forthcoming from them, so they could be omitted as a data source, or replaced with another source. A Plan B could involve abandoning the original research question and data altogether, and finding a more modest and manageable topic with data that is easier to collect.

A Plan B may appear to constitute a failure, but actually the reverse is the case. Knowing that a new approach is needed, and recognising that it is time to switch plans, are valuable skills. It may also be the case that, although the original plan is not yet dead in the water (research as seafaring), a more interesting route has emerged. The ability to notice potential new aspects to research is also a very useful skill. There are many examples of research projects where findings were only discovered either as a result of an initial plan not working, or as a result of the accidental emergence of a new and unexpected aspect. Being alert to all these contingencies shows good observational skills as well as resourcefulness and flexibility. It goes without saying that the ability to adapt and think on your feet is a key workplace skill.

CREATING A SYSTEM

Any project work, academic or otherwise, needs to be organised in a systematic way, including being allocated its own physical (and/or virtual) space. To continue the analogy with other procedural activities such as cooking or furniture construction, a system needs to be sorted before you begin – laying out the ingredients, or counting up the nuts and bolts to make sure everything is present and correct. You need the right tools for the job, and the right elements to build from. Academic research is no different, and, in the case of discourse analysis, you might have a range of different types of data to accommodate – for example, some interview data, some images,

>me newspaper articles and so on. Not only do the different data >urces need a space of their own, but also the originals need to be opied and stored somewhere securely so that if working copies are >st, there is a back-up. The space for each source could be a tradi-onal card or plastic file, a computer-based file and folder system of our own making, or ready-made storage tools such as Zotero (free) >r NVivo (expensive, but if you are studying at a college or univer-ity, they may have an institutional licence).

In the paragraph above, the phrase 'the right tools for the job' was ised, and, in the case of academic research, these are the tools you vill be using for constructing your analysis. You fashion these tools rom reading different academic sources – such as this book – that explain how academic subject fields are concerned with particu-ar research questions, and with particular ways of answering those questions. It has been emphasised throughout this book that good esearch uses approaches that fit the research question, and that can nean drawing on ideas from more than one academic field. The vay to customise your analytical toolkit, then, is to do plenty of eading of academic articles and books so that you can acknowledge vhere the elements of your toolkit have come from.

JSING SECONDARY SOURCES

The reading that you do to inform you about your chosen research copic is termed **secondary sources**. Your various data sources are seen as 'primary sources' in that potentially they contain direct evi-dence for answering your research question, while academic books and articles help to inform the direction of your research rather than answering any question directly. Your reading of secondary sources is typically built into something called a **literature review**, which confusingly is neither about literary texts nor a review in any ordinary sense of the word. Instead, the word 'literature' is used in its widest sense, to refer to things that are written. And the review is not concerned with evaluation in the sense of TripAdvisor or music journalism, where a reviewer discusses the whole experi-ence or artefact and aims to cover all the different aspects. It is not a case of explaining the whole book or article to someone who may be interested in reading it. The rationale for discussing what you have read is that you will pick out only the ideas or approaches or evidence from the material that has relevance for your study. Relevance is the key.

Just as your data needs to be organised and to have a space of its own, so does your reading. A literature review is not a list of a researcher's reading. It is, rather, a kind of thematic essay, referring to relevant academic material but not on an item-by-item basis. The material needs to be gathered together and referred to according to the themes or approaches covered. For example, a researcher looking at educational achievement with reference to gender and social class would have a wide range of books and articles that are considered relevant. But rather than taking the books and articles one by one, all the material that relates to gender needs to be grouped together, and the same for social class.

It is important in any discussion of secondary sources that material is cited and referenced accurately. A **citation** is used in the body of a thesis where there is a direct quotation from a source, or where there is a discussion of ideas taken from a source. The citation consists of the writer's (or speaker's) name, the date of publication or broadcast, and, for written texts, a page number where the source can be located. A full **reference** is then provided in the form of a list towards the end of the thesis, where the full details of the cited publications can be found. Referencing is an important skill to acquire because a researcher who does not acknowledge when he or she has used another's ideas or words can be accused of plagiarism, which is a serious offence.

There are many accessible guides to referencing and most academic libraries will have their own guidance, including ways to cite and reference multimodal material such as websites and blogs. In addition, academic departments will offer their own guidance on which system to use, as there are alternatives.

RECORD-KEEPING AND NOTE-MAKING

The ability to be accurate and efficient in citing and referencing relies heavily on a researcher's record-keeping and note-making habits. It may seem that, having recently read an article about a chosen topic, it would be easy to remember which part of the article

iscussed a certain aspect. But the reality is that it will soon slip from
memory as your attention turns to other activities. If you then go on
o read further articles about the same topic, it will become less and
ess likely that you will remember where exactly you read about a
articular idea or where a writer used a good turn of phrase to sum
omething up. Hours of wasted time will then ensue while you hunt
hrough endless reams of paper or webpage history logs hunting for
hat elusive piece of text. Worse, you may find it again and refer to
 in your own writing but forget to write down the full reference
etails. Cue more skimming and scanning of material to find the
ight information.

Good record-keeping and note-making are ways to maximise
ime spent on the more important activities of thinking, reading
nd writing. Keeping records and making notes are not simply key
actors in noting details about reading; they can also have a crucial
unction in some types of discourse-analytic observational research,
or example in courtrooms, where recording is forbidden, or in work-
ng with children or other vulnerable groups where recording may
listort or intimidate participants.

Note-making is a skill in its own right, beyond its application
n research contexts. Key factors in good note-making are the abil-
ty to identify the most important pieces of information, and the ability
o recover the ideas or experiences the notes refer to. One way to
mprove note-making skills is to practise the art of **précis**: try sum-
narising a page of ideas or a section of a chapter using only a small
number of words, perhaps in bullet-point format. You could choose
one of the chapters in this book and see if you can précis its contents
o fill no more than a page of notes. Inexperienced note-makers
often write too much, copying out whole chunks of text. The art is
o be minimal, but still identify the central ideas.

Recoverability is the second factor noted above. The notes need
o be understandable, otherwise you are left with a puzzle of your
own making. At the other extreme from copying out whole chunks
of text is the note-maker who is too gnomic, thinking they will
remember what their abbreviations and various codes refer to. One
or two abbreviations work but an extensive shorthand will be difficult to recover (unless it is real shorthand and the user is familiar
with it).

ETHICS

Any research has an effect on the people involved in it. Obviously, if you are planning to investigate some advertising, no individuals are likely to be affected. But any work with people needs to respect the rights of the individuals involved.

Your research should not cause anyone harm. This is particularly relevant when you are planning to work with young children, people with learning difficulties or anyone else who is vulnerable. You need to obtain informed consent from carers or parents. In the UK, in some situations you will need to obtain a DBS (Disclosure and Barring Service) check (formerly called a Criminal Records Bureau (CRB) check). Think about the participants in your study – what will taking part in your research feel like from their perspective? If you are thinking of doing any kind of 'testing', then ask yourself whether this is really necessary.

The principle of **informed consent** means that people who are the subject of research need to have a reasonable idea about what they are letting themselves in for, so you need to be as open as possible about what you are doing, and they need to give their permission for you to use data that resulted from their involvement. Research can sometimes face the problem of the **observer's paradox**, which refers to the fact that the presence of the researcher or researchers giving detailed outlines of their plans can distort the very thing that is being researched. This is a known issue in certain kinds of research, and there is no perfect solution to the problem. You don't need to go into detail about every aspect of your plans, but you do need to explain your methodology to anyone involved. If you are planning to do some recording, the fact that people know they are being recorded shouldn't be a problem if you record for a reasonable amount of time: as time goes on, people become less self-conscious. You don't have to transcribe everything you record. There is more about transcription later in this chapter. If people don't like the experience of participating in your investigation, they have the right to withdraw, with no negative consequences to themselves.

No one in your research should be recognisable or traceable. That means you must not use their real names, or give away their location details or access details, which includes their physical and virtual addresses, phone numbers, or any other personal details.

PECIFIC RESEARCH SKILLS

Having covered a range of aspects that are generic to much research, the following sections focus more specifically on the issues of collection and representation associated with the types of data frequently collected by discourse analysts.

COLLECTING AND REPRESENTING SPOKEN DISCOURSE

There are many different types of spoken language, so how spoken language is collected, and also the best way to present it, really depends on what the research question is. Below are some different types of speech – defined as language using oral-aural channels – that might be collected by discourse analysts. Note that this list is neither comprehensive nor definitive. There is no type of speech that is a priori off limits:

Formal speeches – political speeches, ceremonial speeches such as a wedding speech or funeral oration, spoken presentations such as pupils' 'speaking and listening' assessment . . .

Interviews – e.g. in organisations

Transactional talk – e.g. at service desks

Occupational talk – e.g. the occupational registers used in a particular organisation

Group conversations – e.g. in youth settings

Spontaneous talk – e.g. among school pupils

(Semi) scripted or edited media talk – e.g. press conferences, stand-up comedy routines, TV chat shows, 'reality' TV talk, sports commentaries, educational programmes, documentaries, TV or radio advertising, films . . .

Phone calls, voicemails – e.g. in a call centre, radio phone-ins

Storytelling – e.g. recounting personal experiences

Readings – e.g. to analyse accent features

Spoken diaries – e.g. individuals recording daily routines

Some of these speech genres will be more challenging to collect than others, and some may need several attempts. For example, a TV programme such as a chat show has already been made and broadcast, so collecting it is a matter of recording and transcribing (but of course there are still some complex further decisions about how much to transcribe and which parts to select). However, recording naturally occurring speech involves a range of immediately pragmatic challenges such as how to limit background noise and how to set up recording equipment in as unobtrusive a way as possible (assuming that any ethical issues have been resolved). There is much merit in running a small pilot study where possible, because this will quickly raise any issues that may have derailed the main project if it had gone ahead straight away.

SPEECH AND CONTEXT

As soon as spoken language is represented, decisions have to be made about how much context to provide to do justice to the original. In fact, there is no real way to do justice fully to the original because any representation is not the thing itself. But to understand something of the context that the spoken language was embedded in originally, having a system indicating the physical actions and positions of the participants can be a useful addition. For example, if the data is drawn from a media source such as a TV programme or film, an accompanying storyboard can be helpful. If the setting was a business meeting or school classroom, a diagram showing where participants were sitting can help readers of the research project to understand aspects such as turn-taking and deictic expressions.

Further decisions about which parts of the data collected should be transcribed, and what that transcription should look like, are closely related to the research question and, in turn, the particular aspects under scrutiny. For example, a study of regional accents will require **phonetic** detail, but this would be irrelevant in many other data sources. A transcript of a speech may need details about the speaker's non-verbal behaviour, prosody (aspects such as intonation, volume and pitch) and paralanguage (such as laughter and voice quality), as well as some information about audience behaviour. But all those aspects are linked with how the speech is delivered, nd depending on the focus of the research, it may be much more nportant to focus on what was said rather than on how – in which ase, annotations will be much more about themes than about the naller technical features of language. In the end, it is up to the esearcher to decide where attention is best placed to achieve the right alance and emphasis.

If you do decide that you want to use some technical annotations in a transcription, you do not have to invent your own system s the field of Conversation Analysis (see Chapter 7) has generated ymbols that are frequently used by academics. The main exponent f systems of annotation was Gail Jefferson (1938–2008) and many university departments use versions of her work: for example, see he guidance on the site hosted by Charles Antaki at the University of Loughborough: http://homepages.lboro.ac.uk/~ssca1/notation. itm.

There is also guidance in a number of books, for example in ten Have (1999). If you are studying in a college or university they may have their own guides that you are recommended or even required to follow.

COLLECTING AND REPRESENTING WRITTEN DISCOURSE

Working with written data does not present the same logistical issues but there are some comparable aspects to consider. Note that because there is a section starting on the next page on multimodal discourse, this section will focus on more traditional, paper-based texts, or written material that is available digitally but where its original format was paper-based.

As with spoken discourse, there are many different genres of writing that could potentially form part or all of the data for a discourse-analytic project. Here are some examples:

Written stories (not part of professional publications) – e.g. children's writing

Magazine advertisements – e.g. for products aimed at a particular group

Magazine features – e.g. problem pages, celebrity stories, 'real-life' stories

Special interest publications – e.g. cookery, property

Promotional material – e.g. flyers, freesheets, junk mail

Newspaper articles – e.g. news reports, editorials, features, obituari

Literary texts – e.g. where a particular group is represented theme explored

Comics and graphic novels – as above

Non-fiction texts – as above

Organisational documents – e.g. policy documents, instruction handbooks, business memos, agendas and minutes, written tex from particular occupations such as education, medicine or la

Writing that marks social customs – e.g. greetings cards such as birth day cards

As will be obvious from the list above, collecting writing can pro duce a huge amount of material, so it is especially important to b as specific as possible about what exactly the aim of the researc is. As with any research, focusing tightly on a particular aspec involves a rationale for rejecting other areas, but this is a crucia process. Many research projects struggle from trying to do too much. And it is possible to be creative in thinking about a focus For example, for a project about the ideology of magazines, wha about looking just at the contents page of a range of magazines and imagine that you lived your life in that page: what would your life be all about?

COLLECTING AND REPRESENTING MULTIMODAL DISCOURSE

Multimodal discourse refers to the many forms of digital commu-nication that surround us in contemporary society – for example, SMS, email, social media posts, blogs and vlogs, websites. Such texts are termed multimodal because they have features that have been traditionally associated with speech and writing, but blended in new ways. They are also termed 'hybrid' because of their blended nature.

Digital texts exist alongside, and in relationship to, all the other types of spoken and written texts that have had a longer shelf-life. It may be the case, therefore, that a researcher wants to follow a discourse across multimodal communication but in a conventional format too. An example of this might be a focus on a news story that exists in paper format and also appears on the same newspaper's online site. These different contexts offer very different communication constraints – both **affordances** and **limitations** – and these constraints can produce distinctively different narratives. Another example of a comparative focus might be the way an organisation represents itself internally compared with its outward-facing website.

Digital communication can therefore be studied in its own right but also as an extension of an individual's, group's or organisation's communication output.

COLLECTING AND REPRESENTING VISUAL DISCOURSE

Visual discourse requires its own methods of data collection. Capturing an image has become considerably easier with the advent of high-quality camera tools on smartphones; and these also have video capacity, as has been evident from the number of times ordinary members of the public have recorded events as they unfolded. Examples of such 'citizen journalism' now feature regularly in mainstream news coverage.

There is considerable potential for exploring interesting questions about how we use visual signs and symbols and how they form a part of the discourses we inhabit. For example, the front entrance of an organisation in all its aspects – the fabrics of construction, the use of colour, the displays, the ways that incomers are channelled and so on – speaks volumes about that institution's ideologies. Internally, too, there are symbols at work in how people and products are organised: for example, some well-known toy shops differentiate strongly between toys aimed at boys and girls by the use of colour coding, endorsing gendered discourses about the appropriate worlds to aspire to, for young children, on the basis of their sex. However, collecting images needs to be done carefully, with support and guidance from the members of academic staff involved in project supervision. Just as researchers need to be ethical in the way they treat others, so it important for them to think about their own welfare.

HANDLING MULTIPLE DATA SOURCES

There have already been some suggestions about possible connec tions between different data sources, and a carefully focused researc question answered by evidence from more than one source can b richly satisfying. But the different data sources need tying togethe otherwise they can become unwieldy. It is important to think abou what they add to the overall debate. For example, what might a image of the front entrance of a main university building add to a analysis of the front pages of its prospectus (online or paper-based, c both)? Are there themes that are shared across these different text or contradicted?

A good analysis will avoid a serial approach, where texts are ana lysed one after another; instead it will move between them in pursui of a range of ideas that arise from studying them.

USING COMPUTER-BASED RESEARCH TOOLS

Depending on the nature of the data being collected, it is wort exploring how computer-based search tools could take some of th labour out of building an analysis. Because it is possible to build a collection of texts into a digitised corpus, computer tools can enabl researchers to search and find examples of terms in seconds, and there fore spot patterns that would have taken a human several hours o tedious work. This does not require expensive purchases or high level of technical ability. For example, the search tool in Microsoft Worc enables searches of written text, so as long as any text has been worc processed, this can be searched for repeated occurrences of terms. There are also free or very cheap search tools available online – fo example, WordSmith. Again, if you are studying as part of a college or university course it is worth exploring what is available in your department, or as part of the virtual learning environment across the wider university.

There are also existing corpora, often hosted by academic departments, that can be searched cost-free to explore how particular words and phrases are used in different types of text. Examples of commonly used corpora include the British National Corpus (BNC) at Oxford University (www.natcorp.ox.ac.uk) and the Corpus of Global Web-Based English (GloWbE), based at Brigham Young University in the USA (http://corpus.byu.edu/glowbe).

If you are not familiar with corpus work, go to one of these sites and search for the use of a specific word. You will see the results expressed as a set of lines with your chosen term in context: this is known as a **concordance**. This can help with discourse-analytic work because it enables a researcher to see how a term they might have in their data is commonly used either elsewhere or in similar types of text (corpora enable you to see the sources that are drawn from, for any searched words).

WRITING STYLES AND READERSHIP ISSUES

The question of writing styles has been included here rather than in the general section of this chapter because, to some extent, the style adopted in research papers and dissertations is determined by the academic department the researcher belongs to. To make statements that advise on universal approaches is therefore a little problematic.

Aside from the caveat given, there are some aspects of writing about discourse that are worth considering, regardless of the researcher's academic affiliation. Discourse-analytic work needs to pay particular attention to issues of organisation, particularly if several sources of data are being used. Data would normally be placed in an appendix, but it may be that extracts from the data benefit from being brought forward into the main discussion, as well as living in an appendix. Depending on the complexity and density of the material being analysed, it can be hard work as a reader to have to constantly refer to the back of a thesis just to locate a few words or phrases.

Thinking about how a reader will experience the analysis is an important consideration. Readers need to be carefully guided through the analysis. This is sometimes forgotten by academic writers who have spent a very long time with the same data, so fail to grasp how much needs explaining to someone coming new to it.

There are also some simple issues of layout that could be though
through. For example, a list of examples or a set of bullet points
a box drawn around some text can sometimes aid readability whe
the alternative – a long chunk of continuous prose – needs mud
more processing.

Finally, we need to debunk some myths about the question
pronoun choice for the researcher's own narrative. Sometimes st
dents express a dilemma about a choice of writing style, seeing it as
choice between supposedly subjective and objective representation
The examples often quoted are the use of 'I' in expressions such
'I believe that' as 'subjective', and the use of passive constructions i
expressions such as 'it is believed that' as 'objective'. This is actuall
a false choice that unfortunately maintains a stereotype that to be
really 'pure' academic a writer must use supposedly objective expres
sions. This is a distorted and over-simplified picture.

There's nothing wrong with using 'I' now and then but a piec
of writing peppered with 'I think' and 'I believe' can sound rathe
under-confident, as if the writer's statements alone are not indica
tive enough of their perspective. On the other hand, it's odd to rea
an analysis where the writer appears not to have had any part in th
proceedings, which is the effect created where expressions such a
'the view was taken that . . .'.

The best, neutral-sounding style is a kind of statement style
which you have seen exemplified throughout this book. A statemen
style makes statements about a text or an idea, for example:

> 'this part of the text suggests that . . .'
> 'this idea is only partly true because . . .'

Statements can also be phrased tentatively, which is important giver
that many different readings of a text and many different views abou
discourse are possible:

> 'this may mean that . . .'
> 'it could be the case that . . .'

A statement style uses a third-person narrative approach and, as you
saw in Chapter 8 of this book, third-person narrative can be a very

useful, flexible choice. It creates an observational tone but one within which it is still possible to construct your own perspective. Here is a statement style in action, from the beginning of this chapter:

If discourse is about doing something – performing a role, expressing an identity, acting out a script, constructing a reality, creating meanings – then it would be odd to come to the end of a book on discourse without thinking about doing something with discourse as a researcher.

REFERENCES AND
FURTHER READING

In the list below, an asterisk placed against a text indicates that it
also recommended for further reading. Some additional suggestion
for further reading can be found after the references.

REFERENCES

Aitchison, J. (2001). *Language Change: Progress or Decay?* Oxford: Oxfor
  University Press.
Atkinson, M. (1984). *Our Masters' Voices: The Language and Body-Language*
  Politics. London: Routledge.
Austin, J.L. (1980). *How To Do Things With Words*. Oxford: Oxford Universit
  Press.
Baker, J. (2014). *Longbourn*. London: Black Swan.
*Baker, P. (2008). *Sexed Texts*. London: Equinox.
Bakhtin, M.M. (1992). *The Dialogic Imagination: Four Essays*. Austin, TX
  University of Texas Press.
Barker, C. and Galasinski, D. (2001). *Cultural Studies and Discourse Analysis:*
  Dialogue on Language and Identity. London: Sage.
Barnes, C. and Mercer, G. (2010). *Exploring Disability: A Sociological Introduction*
  2nd edn. Cambridge: Polity Press.
Beasley, V. (2009). 'Between Touchstones and Touch Screens: What Counts a
  Contemporary Political Rhetoric?' In A. Lunsford, K. Wilson and R. Eberly
  (eds), *The Sage Handbook of Rhetorical Studies*. London: Sage, pp. 587–604.

ck, C.T. (2006). 'Pentadic Cartography: Mapping Birth Trauma Narratives'. *Qualitative Health Research* 16(4), 453–66.

Benwell, B. and Stokoe, E. (2006). *Discourse and Identity*. Edinburgh: Edinburgh University Press.

erger, P. and Luckmann, T. (1991). *The Social Construction of Reality*. London: Penguin.

erridge, V. (2013). *Demons: Our Changing Attitudes to Alcohol, Tobacco and Drugs*. Oxford: Oxford University Press.

erube, A. (1996). 'Intellectual Desire'. *GLQ: A Journal of Lesbian and Gay Studies* 3(1), 139–57.

illig, M. (1995). *Banal Nationalism*. London: Sage.

oyd, W. (2010). *Ordinary Thunderstorms*. London: Bloomsbury.

rown, A. (2001). 'Hoffman's Tale', online *Guardian* article. Available at: www.theguardian.com/books/2001/apr/28/internationaleducationnews.socialsciences (accessed 19 January 2017).

rown, P. and Levinson, S. (1987). *Politeness: Some Universals in Language Usage*. Cambridge: Cambridge University Press.

rown, R. (2013). *Everything for Sale? The Marketisation of UK Higher Education*. London: Routledge.

urke, K. (1966). *Language as Symbolic Action*. Berkeley, CA: University of California Press.

Cameron, D. (1995). *Verbal Hygiene*. London: Routledge.

Carter, A. (1995). *The Bloody Chamber*. London: Vintage Classics.

Carter, R. (2004). *Language and Creativity: The Art of Common Talk*. London: Routledge.

Carter, R. and Nash, W. (1990). *Seeing Through Language*. London: Wiley.

Carter, R. and Goddard, A. (2015). *How to Analyse Texts: A Toolkit for Students of English*. London: Routledge.

Chandler, D. (2006). 'Identities under Construction'. In J. Maybin (ed.), *The Art of English*. Maidenhead: Open University Press, pp. 303–11.

Chandler, D. (2007). *Semiotics: The Basics*. 2nd edn. London: Routledge.

Charteris-Black, J. (2013). *Analysing Political Speeches: Rhetoric, Discourse and Metaphor*. Basingstoke: Palgrave Macmillan.

Clark, K. (1998). 'The Linguistics of Blame: Representations of Women in *The Sun*'s Reporting of Crimes of Sexual Violence'. In D. Cameron (ed.), *The Feminist Critique of Language*. London: Routledge, pp. 183–97.

Coates, J. (2003). *Men Talk: Stories in the Making of Masculinities*. Oxford: Blackwell.

Crowley, T. (1989). *The Politics of Discourse: The Standard Language Question in British Cultural Debates*. London: Macmillan.

Crystal, D. (2001). *Language and the Internet*. Cambridge: Cambridge University Press.

Cutler, T. (2016). 'Talking Points: 10 Things to Take Away from this Weeken 1: Semenya's Dominance Fuels Debate over her Eligibility', *i*, 18 April.

Davies, T. (1997). *Humanism (the New Critical Idiom)*. London: Routledge.

de Boinod, J. (2005). *The Meaning of Tingo and Other Extraordinary Words Fro Around the World*. London: Penguin.

Duffy, C.A. (2010). *The World's Wife*. London: Picador.

Edley, N. and Wetherell, M. (1997). 'Jockeying for Position: The Constructio of Masculine Identities'. *Discourse and Society* 8(2), 203–17.

Empson, W. [1930] (2014). *Seven Types of Ambiguity*. London: Chatto Windus.

Engel, M. (2011). 'Why do some Americanisms irritate people?' *BBC Ne online*. Available at: www.bbc.co.uk/news/14130942 (accessed 19 Janua 2017).

★Fairclough, N. (2010). *Critical Discourse Analysis*. London: Routledge.

Fisher, P. and Freshwater, D. (2014). 'Methodology and Mental Illnes Resistance and Restorying'. *Journal of Psychiatric and Mental Health Nursi* 21, 197–205.

Fowler, R. (1986). *Linguistic Criticism*. Oxford: Oxford University Press.

Frank, A. (1995). *The Wounded Storyteller: Body, Illness and Ethics*. Londor University of Chicago Press.

Friedan, B. (2010). *The Feminine Mystique*. London: Penguin Classics.

Furedi, F. (2009). 'Now is the age of the discontented', *The Times Higher*, June 4 Available at: www.timeshighereducation.com/features/now-is-the-age-of the-discontented/406780.article (accessed 19 January 2017).

Gee, J.P. (1990). *Social Linguistics and Literacies: Ideology in Discourses, Critic Perspectives on Literacy and Education*. London: Routledge.

Gershenson, O. and Penner, B. (2009). *Ladies and Gents: Public Toilets an Gender*. Philadelphia, PA: Temple University Press.

Gibbs, R. (1994). *The Poetics of Mind*. Cambridge: Cambridge University Press

Gibbs, R. (ed.) (2008). *The Cambridge Handbook of Metaphor and Though* Cambridge: Cambridge University Press.

Goddard, A. (2005). *Being Online*. PhD thesis, University of Nottingham.

Goddard, A. (2011). '"Type You Soon!" A Stylistic Approach to Languag Use in a Virtual Learning Environment'. *Language and Literature* 20(3) 184–200.

★Goddard, A. and Geesin, B. (2011). *Language and Technology*. London Routledge.

Goffman, E. (1969). *The Presentation of Self in Everyday Life*. London: Penguin.

Goffman, E. (1974). *Frame Analysis*. Harmondsworth: Penguin.

Gott, M. (2005). *Sexuality, Sexual Health and Ageing*. Maidenhead: Oper University Press.

Grant, D., Hardy, C., Oswick, C. and Putnam, L. (2004). *The Sage Handbook of Organizational Discourse*. London: Sage.

Grech, S. (2015). *Disability and Poverty in the Global South: Renegotiating Development in Guatemala*. Basingstoke: Palgrave Macmillan.

Grice, H.P. (1975). 'Logic and Conversation'. *Syntax and Semantics* 3, 41–58.

Gumperz, J. (1982). *Discourse Strategies*. Cambridge: Cambridge University Press.

Gumperz, J. (1983). *Language and Social Identity.* Cambridge: Cambridge University Press.

Gumperz, J. (1996). *Rethinking Linguistic Relativity*. Cambridge: Cambridge University Press.

Hall, S. (1986). 'Encoding/Decoding'. In S. Hall, A. Lowe and P. Willis (eds), *Culture, Media, Language: Working Papers in Cultural Studies, 1972–79*. London: Hutchinson, pp. 128–38.

Hall, S. (1996). 'The Question of Cultural Identity'. In S. Hall, D. Held, D. Hubert and K. Thompson (eds), *Modernity: An Introduction to Modern Societies*. Malden, MA: Blackwell, pp. 595–6.

Hoffman, E. (2008). *Lost in Translation: A Life in a New Language*. London: Vintage Books.

Jones, O. (2011). *Chavs: The Demonization of the Working Class*. London: Verso.

Kachru, B. (1990). *The Alchemy of English: The Spread, Functions and Models of Non-Native Englishes*. Urbana, IL: University of Illinois Press.

Kim, H. and Elder, C. (2009). 'Understanding Aviation English as a Lingua Franca: Perceptions of Korean Aviation Personnel'. *Australian Review of Applied Linguistics* 32(3), 1–17.

Kulick, D. and Rydström, J. (2015). *Loneliness and Its Opposite: Sex, Disability, and the Ethics of Engagement*. Durham, NC: Duke University Press.

Labov, W. (1972a). 'The Social Motivation of a Sound Change'. In W. Labov (ed.), *Sociolinguistics Patterns*. Philadelphia, PA: University of Philadelphia Press, pp. 1–42.

Labov, W. (1972b). *Language in the Inner City: Studies in Black English Vernacular*. Philadelphia, PA: University of Philadelphia Press.

Lakoff, G. (1987). *Women, Fire and Dangerous Things*. Chicago, IL: University of Chicago Press.

Lakoff, G. and Johnson, M. (1980). *Metaphors We Live By*. Chicago, IL: University of Chicago Press.

Lakoff, R. (1975). *Language and Woman's Place*. Oxford: Oxford University Press.

Laurel, B. (1993). *Computers as Theatre*. Reading, MA: Addison-Wesley.

Lave, J. and Wenger, E. (1991). *Situated Learning*. Cambridge: Cambridge University Press.

Mangham, I. (1996). 'Some Consequences of Taking Gareth Morgan Seriously'. In D. Grant and C. Oswick (eds), *Metaphor and Organizations*. London: Sage, pp. 21–36.

Mayr, A. (2008). *Language and Power: An Introduction to Institutional Discourse*. London: Continuum.

*Mills, S. (2004). *Discourse (the New Critical Idiom series)*. London: Routledge.

Milroy, J. and Milroy, L. (1993). *Real English: The Grammar of English Dialects in the British Isles*. London: Routledge.

Milroy, J. and Milroy, L. (1998). *Authority in Language: Investigating Language Prescription and Standardisation*. London: Routledge.

Molesworth, M., Scullion, R. and Nixon, E. (2010). *The Marketisation of Higher Education and the Student as Consumer*. London: Routledge.

*Morgan, G. (1986). *Images of Organization*. London: Sage.

Mort, F. (2000). *Dangerous Sexualities*. London: Routledge.

Moulaert, T. and Biggs, S. (2016). 'International and European Policy on Work and Retirement: Reinventing Critical Perspectives on Active Ageing and Mature Subjectivity'. *Human Relations* 66(1), 23–43.

Naisbitt, J. (1982). *Megatrends*. New York: Warner.

Nelson, M. (2000). 'A Corpus-Based Study of Business English and Business English Teaching Materials'. Unpublished PhD thesis. Manchester: University of Manchester Press.

Ortony, A. (ed.) (1993). *Metaphor and Thought*. Cambridge: Cambridge University Press.

Peel, E. (2014). '"The Living Death of Alzheimer's" versus "Take a Walk to Keep Dementia at Bay": Representations of Dementia in Print Media and Carer Discourse'. *Sociology of Health and Illness* 36(6), 885–901.

Pope, R. (1994). *Textual Intervention: Critical and Creative Strategies for Literary Studies*. London: Routledge.

Rose, N. (1985). *The Psychological Complex: Psychology, Politics and Society in England, 1869–1939*. London: Routledge.

Rhys, J. (2000 [1966]). *The Wide Sargasso Sea*. London: Penguin Classics.

Rutten, K. (2011). 'Academic Discourse and Literacy Narratives as "Equipment for Living"'. *CLCWeb: Comparative Literature and Culture* 13(4), http://dx.doi.org/10.7771/1481-4374.1880.

Sacks, H. (1995). *Lectures on Conversation*. Volumes I and II. Edited by G. Jefferson. Oxford: Blackwell.

Sapir, E. (1929). 'The Status of Linguistics as a Science'. *Language* 5, 207–14.

*Saraceni, M. (2010). *The Relocation of English: Shifting Paradigms in a Global Era*. London: Palgrave Macmillan.

Schegloff, E. (1979). 'Identification and Recognition in Telephone Conversation Openings'. In G. Psathas (ed.), *Everyday Language*. New York: Irvington, pp. 22–78.

Schiffrin, D. (1994). *Approaches to Discourse*. Oxford: Blackwell.

Shakespeare, T. (2014). *Disability Rights and Wrongs Revisited*. 2nd edn. London: Routledge.

Sherwin, A. (2016). 'Forget Medicine and be a Game Designer', *i*, 13 September.

Shildrick, M. (2004). 'Silencing Sexuality: The Regulation of the Disabled Body'. In J. Carabine (ed.), *Sexualities: Personal Lives and Social Policy*. Bristol: Open University Press, pp. 123–57.

Shildrick, M. (2012). *Dangerous Discourses of Disability, Subjectivity and Sexuality*. New York: Palgrave Macmillan.

*Simpson, P. (1993). *Language, Ideology and Point of View*. London: Routledge.

Simpson, P. (2004). *Stylistics: A Resource Book for Students*. London: Routledge.

Southey, R. (1831). *Sir Thomas More, or, Colloquies on the Progress and Prospects of Society*. London: J. Murray.

Spender, D. (1980). *Man Made Language*. London: Routledge.

Sperber, D. and Wilson, D. (1986). *Relevance: Communication and Cognition*. Oxford: Blackwell.

Stoegner, K. and Wodak, R. (2016). '"The Man Who Hated Britain": The Discursive Construction of "National Unity" in the Daily Mail'. *Critical Discourse Studies* 13(2), 193–209.

Stone, A.R. (1995). *The War of Desire and Technology at the Close of the Machine Age*. Cambridge, MA: MIT Press.

*Sturken, M. and Cartwright, L. (2001). *Practices of Looking: An Introduction to Visual Culture*. New York: Oxford University Press.

Swain, S. (1988). *Great Housewives of Art*. New York: HarperCollins.

Swales, J. (1998). *Other Floors, Other Voices: A Textography of a Small University Building*. London: Routledge.

Tannen, D. (1981). 'Indirectness in Discourse: Ethnicity as Conversational Style'. *Discourse Processes* 4(3), 221–38.

*Tannen, D. (ed.) (1993). *Framing in Discourse*. Oxford: Oxford University Press.

ten Have, P. (1999). *Doing Conversation Analysis*. London: Sage.

Thurlow, C. (2003). 'Generation Txt?: The Sociolinguistics of Young People's Text-Messaging'. *Discourse Analysis Online*. Available at: http://extra.shu.ac.uk/daol/articles/v1/n1/a3/thurlow2002003-01.html (accessed 19 January 2017).

*Tietze, S., Cohen, L. and Musson, G. (2003). *Understanding Organizations Through Language*. London: Sage.

*Toolan, M. (2001). *Narrative: A Critical Linguistic Introduction*. London: Routledge.

*Toye, R. (2013). *Rhetoric: A Very Short Introduction*. Oxford: Oxford University Press.

Trudgill, P. (1999). 'Standard English: What It Isn't'. In T. Bex and R. Watts (eds), *Standard English: The Widening Debate*. London: Routledge, pp. 117–28.

Turkle, S. (1995). *Life on the Screen*. New York: Simon & Schuster.

*Van Dijk, T. (2015). 'Critical Discourse Analysis'. In D. Tannen, H. Hamilton and D. Schiffrin (eds), *Handbook of Discourse Analysis*. 2nd edn. Chichester: Wiley Blackwell, pp. 352–71.

Whorf, B.L. (1940). 'Science and Linguistics'. *MIT Technology Review* 213–14.

Wittgenstein, L. (1922). *Tractatus Logico-Philosophicus*. Austria.

Wodak, R. (2015). *The Politics of Fear: What Right-Wing Populist Discour Mean*. London: Sage.

WEBSITE-ONLY REFERENCES

Adbusters (this link is to their 'spoof ads'):
www.adbusters.org/spoofads
(Accessed in March 2017)

Boom Chicago's 'Zwarte Piet' rap:
www.youtube.com/watch?v=vyTW-S0yTiI
(Accessed in March 2017)

University of Leicester School of Psychology – overview of Jefferson transcriptic conventions:
www2.le.ac.uk/departments/psychology/research/child-mental-health/cara-1 faqs/jefferson
(Accessed in March 2017)

The Living Handbook of Narratology – a website devoted to this area:
www.lhn.uni-hamburg.de
(Accessed in March 2017)

Michael Nelson's Business English Lexis Site:
http://users.utu.fi/micnel/business_english_lexis_site.htm
(Accessed in March 2017)

TED talks:
www.ted.com
(Accessed in March 2017)

ADDITIONAL SUGGESTIONS FOR FURTHER READING

Barker, C. (2004). *Cultural Studies: Theory and Practice*. London: Sage.

Barthes, R. (1972). *Mythologie*s. London: Vintage.

Beal, J. (2010). *An Introduction to Regional Englishes*. Edinburgh: Edinburgh University Press.

rtens, H. (2001). *Literary Theory: The Basics*. London: Routledge.

ommaert, J. (2005). *Discourse (Key Topics in Sociolinguistics)*. Cambridge: Cambridge University Press.

urke, K. (1978). 'Questions and Answers about the Pentad'. *College Composition and Communication* 29(4), 330–5.

ameron, D. (ed.) (1998). *The Feminist Critique of Language*. London: Routledge.

ameron, D. and Kulick, D. (2003). *Language and Sexuality*. Cambridge: Cambridge University Press.

arter, R. and McCarthy, M. (1997). *Exploring Spoken English*. Cambridge: Cambridge University Press.

hilton, P. (2004). *Analysing Political Discourse: Theory and Practice*. London: Routledge.

obley, P. (2014). *Narrative (the New Critical Idiom)*. 2nd edn. London: Routledge.

ockcroft, R. and Cockcroft, S. (2005). *Persuading People: An Introduction to Rhetoric*. London: Palgrave Macmillan.

uller, J. (2011). *Literary Theory: A Very Short Introduction*. Oxford: Oxford University Press.

airclough, N. (2003). *Analysing Discourse: Textual Analysis for Social Research*. London: Routledge.

ineman, S. (2011). *Organizing Age*. Oxford: Oxford University Press.

ee, J.P. (1999). *An Introduction to Discourse Analysis*. London: Routledge.

oddard, A. (2002). *The Language of Advertising*. London: Routledge.

oddard, A. and Mean, L. (2009). *Language and Gender*. London: Routledge.

arris, R. and Rampton, B. (eds) (2003). *The Language, Ethnicity and Race Reader*. London: Routledge.

olliday, A., Hyde, M. and Kullman, J. (2004). *Intercultural Communication: An Advanced Resource Book*. London: Routledge.

aworski, A. and Coupland, N. (1999). *The Discourse Reader*. London: Routledge.

enkins, J. (2003). *World Englishes: A Resource Book for Students*. London: Routledge.

eller, R. (2013). *Doing Discourse Research: An Introduction for Social Scientists*. London: Sage.

oester, A. (2006). *Investigating Workplace Discourse*. London: Routledge.

övecses, Z. (2010). *Metaphor: A Practical Introduction*. 2nd edn. New York: Oxford University Press.

eyers, G. (2010). *Discourse of Blogs and Wikis*. London: Continuum Press.

ennycook, A. (1998). *English and the Discourses of Colonialism*. London: Routledge.

collon, R. and Scollon, S. (2003). *Discourses in Place: Language in the Material World*. London: Routledge.

Strauss, S. and Feiz, P. (2014). *Discourse Analysis: Putting our Worlds into Wor*
New York: Routledge.

Thurlow, C., Lengel, L. and Tomic, A. (2004). *Computer Mediated Communicatic Social Interaction and the Internet*. London: Sage.

Wodak, R. and Meyer, M. (2009). *Methods of Critical Discourse Analysis*. 2nd ed
London: Sage.

GLOSSARY/INDEX

On the following pages you will find a combined glossary and index. The key terms that are in bold in the book are defined here, along with a page reference indicating the first occurrence of the term in question. Sometimes there is more than one page reference, showing that there is detailed discussion of the term on more than one occasion in the book.

active and passive voice A verb that is in the active voice has a subject that is carrying out the action of the verb – e.g. in 'she learned Spanish', 'she' is the subject and 'learned' is an active verb; 'Spanish' is the object, undergoing the action. If this is turned into the passive voice, the word order changes to 'Spanish was learned by her', moving the previous object to the front of the sentence and changing the form of the verb. In the passive construction, the person doing the action is expressed via an agent phrase ('by her') but can be left out. 135–7

adjacency The positioning of elements in an interaction, so that one follows on from another, although they don't have to occur immediately afterwards. Elements in an adjacency relationship often occur in pairs – e.g. greetings are usually reciprocal, questions are followed by answers, etc. 102, 123

affordances   See **communication constraints**. 181

agent phrase   In a passive sentence, an agent phrase identifies wh[...] is carrying out the action of the verb, but this can be left o[...] without making the sentence or utterance incomprehensible. 1[...]

analogy   A comparison between one thing and another to explain [...] clarify some aspects of the first thing being examined. 3

anthropologist   Anthropology is the study of cultures and subcultur[...] Traditionally anthropologists studied 'foreign' or exotic cu[...] tures. More recent anthropology is interested in studying (su[...] cultures within local society. 24

antimetabole   The repetition of elements but using a different wor[...] order – e.g. John F. Kennedy's famous 'Ask not what your cou[...] try can do for you, but ask what you can do for your country'. 8

antithesis   The use of opposites – e.g. references to imprisonme[...] and freedom, or ignorance and knowledge. 85, 92

arbitrary   Having no real connection beyond that of social conventio[...] 26, 38, 40   *Slang   (made up language)*

biological determinism   The strongest (if rare) form of biologic[...] determinism would suggest that all aspects of human and soci[...] activity are the direct result of biology. The suggestion tha[...] human behaviour can be explained by our genes is an example o[...] biological determinism. 161

bricolage   The art of putting different elements together in a creativ[...] way. It suggests the idea of using those materials that are at hand[...] rather than having a grand design plan. The term was originall[...] French and referred to the construction of buildings, but it ha[...] been adopted in academic fields to describe creating artistic arte[...] facts, including texts. 71

bureaucracy   A type of organisation that adopts a clear and rigi[...] system of rules and procedures to achieve its goals. Often use[...] derogatorily suggesting overly complicated and unnecessary admin[...] istration. In political terms, bureaucracy is the collective term fo[...] non-elected officials who run government. 62–3

citation   Identifying a source in the body of a thesis by referring to [...] writer's name and the date of the publication. If a quotation is used[...] a page number for locating the quotation is also necessary. 174

codified   Formalised and written down, with patterns of usage[...] identified. 156

ommodity Something that can be bought and sold. Traditionally commodities were objects or products that could be traded. However, more recently the term applies to a range of services (e.g. financial, leisure, personal). 3, 57

ommunication constraints A term devised by Goffman to describe the shaping factors that affect communication, particularly the cultural conventions of the group involved, and the technical possibilities of the medium and channel chosen. Communication constraints consist of **affordances** – aspects that are enabled by the choice of a particular type of communication – and **limitations** – the aspects that are not available or not fully realisable. 124, 181

ommunity of practice A group of practitioners who have a common interest in sharing knowledge and expertise about a particular activity. The group will meet – virtually or in face-to-face settings – with the explicit aim of exploring their own and wider practice in their area of interest. 5–8

omplaint tradition The idea that complaining about people's language use is part of a strategy to deny others' claims to power. 157

omputer-mediated communication Communication between human beings via the instrumentality of computers. 58, 117

oncordance A set of lines from a language corpus showing how the searched word occurred in a range of sources. 183

onduit A channel for carrying (conducting) something. 60, 112

onnotations The range of meanings that are invoked when a word or phrase is used. Connotative meanings are sometimes contrasted with denotation, i.e. the literal meanings of words, although that distinction is not always so clear cut. The concepts of denotation and connotation are most closely associated with the work of Roland Barthes. 10, 27, 30, 33, 41, 60, 66, 69–70, 88

onsumption Refers to buying or otherwise consuming products or services on an individual or more collective scale. Patterns of consumption identify the macro-level trends in what commodities are bought. 3

ontextualisation convention The schema or model that people have in their minds of how different types of interaction are likely to work. 104

ontextualisation cue A cue or signal of how people in interactions are understanding the context of the conversation they are in. 104–5

ecoded   Decoding refers to the ways that audiences process information and ideas from spoken and written texts. There is not necessarily a one-to-one correspondence between what is meant by the producer of a text (**encoding**) and the meanings taken from the same text when it is being decoded. 43, 112

eductive   A theory-led approach to guide understanding of what is observed on the ground. Sometimes called a 'top-down' approach working from an abstract or theoretical statement which is subsequently tested by collecting data that either confirms or discredits the original proposition. 64

eep metaphors   Metaphors that are deeply ingrained in language and that frame our basic understandings of the world. They are 'deep' precisely because they do not even appear to be metaphorical. Deep metaphors give rise to a more extensive range of surface metaphors. 65

eictics   Words and phrases that are used for indicating aspects of the narrative such as the location of characters in fictive spaces and how the time frame should be understood. Deictic expressions are those that 'point out' – for example 'here', 'there', 'in the house', 'on the street', 'yesterday, 'tomorrow'. 134

eliberative rhetoric   Rhetorical strategies that are specifically designed to persuade people, such as those found in advertising. 74, 76

emagogue   Someone who tries to rally the support of crowds by appealing to popular sentiments and emotions, rather than logical arguments. 75

eterminism   A deterministic view of language is that it is impossible for people to think beyond the parameters of the language that is available to them. 25–6

ialectologist   Someone who collects and studies examples of regional language. 155

ialogic   With reference to education, an approach that involves discussion among learners and with the teacher (rather than being formally instructed). 29, 45

idactic   With reference to education, having a strong focus on instruction (rather than, for example, learning by doing). 45

irect speech   A form of speech presentation in which the narrator reports some speech by reproducing the exact words uttered by a character, usually enclosed in quotation marks and introduced by a reporting clause such as 'he said'. Reporting clauses are a[so] called 'quotatives'. 114, 142

discipline Academic subjects of study are often referred to [as] disciplines – e.g. Psychology, Linguistics, Geography. Disciplin[es] are often further subdivided into sub-disciplines (e.g. Psycholo[gy] has sub-disciplines in Cognitive Psychology, Community Psych[o]logy and so on). Although there is always disagreement, academ[ics] working within a discipline will broadly share understandings [of] the area of study that they are interested in. 3, 10, 38, 55, 56, [6]0, 126, 137, 159–60, 165

discourse community A group of people who have a shar[ed] understanding about the norms, style and purposes of their com[m]unication. Examples include occupational and organisatio[nal] groups or those with a specialised interest in a topic like vid[eo] gaming or health and fitness. Members of a discourse communi[ty] may relate in particular ways to the language used in that the[y] may be producers or consumers of such discourses. 5–8

Discourse-Historical Approach (DHA) An approach which com[-]bines critical discourse analysis with insights from historic[al] perspectives. 93

discursive resources At the macro cultural level, these are the linguist[ic] and wider cultural knowledges that frame and inform how phe[-]nomena are experienced and understood. At the individual lev[el] such resources refer to the verbal, interactional and non-verb[al] practices that people bring to bear in communication behaviour. 6

Dramatistic Pentad An analytical framework devised by Kennet[h] Burke, the influential American critic and rhetorical analyst. 95–

ellipsis The omission of words or phrases which can be under[-]stood from the context – e.g. 'want some tea?' ('do you' has bee[n] ellipted). 116, 122

encoded Concerned with the production of messages in the form [of] spoken and written texts that are subsequently **decoded** as the[y] are consumed by audiences. 28, 43, 48–9, 55, 61

English as a lingua franca (ELF) The use of the English language for pur[-]poses of communication by speakers of different first languages. 158

Enlightenment A period of history and an intellectual movement fro[m] the eighteenth century characterised by the rejection of religiou[s] rule in favour of rational and scientific approaches to understandin[g] the physical and social world. 160

deictic rhetoric Rhetorical strategies that depend on display, for example in a ceremonial speech. 74, 76

essence/essentialism (as in identity) The idea that manifestations of identity can be explained by some inner core or attribute. Making the claim that motherhood is a natural attribute of all females is an example of an essentialist explanation. 160–1

ethnographic The systematic study of people, places and cultures from the viewpoint of an insider to that culture. The term ethnography can refer to both the methods of study and the 'report' that is the end result of such study. 8, 64

ethos In the field of rhetoric, the idea of the reputational power of a speaker – e.g. that of a well-known and respected public figure. 75–6

etymology The study of the origin of words and how their meanings were established and may have changed over time. 30, 108

euphemism An indirect form of language that enables speakers or writers to avoid mentioning something unpleasant, offensive or problematic. For example, 'passing on' might be used instead of 'dying'. 19, 28

face In Face Theory, the idea that we all have a public self-image that we need to project and protect. 108, 123

face management The management of our public image. 108

face-threatening act In Face Theory, something that threatens a person's self-image. 108

false consciousness A central idea in Marxist theory to describe how those who are oppressed by an unequal economic system falsely believe that the very system that oppresses them is actually fair. Marxists would claim that the popular claim that working hard leads to wealth is an example of false consciousness because it is unlikely without being born into wealth in the first place. 52

feminism Political movements advocating the rights of women to achieve equality of the sexes. 27–30, 43, 51, 145

figurative Language that goes beyond literal meaning to express an idea. Metaphor is an aspect of figurative language; so are idioms. An idiom is an expression whose meaning is not dependent on the meanings of the individual words it contains – for example, saying that someone 'has a chip on their shoulder' or that they are 'turning over a new leaf'. These sayings use everyday words but have particular meanings as whole expressions. 54, 82

speech. The field is closely associated with the work of Joh Gumperz, who focused on processes of inference. 104-6, 124

interdisciplinary   Academic work that borrows theories and metho from two or more established academic disciplines. 12

international English   Forms of English that are used around th world, including 'New Englishes' or 'World Englishes' as well 'English as a lingua franca'. 18, 157

intersectional   Identities are said to be multiple because peop identify with and are categorised along several different axes identity. For example, someone identifying as a white Polis woman manifests an identity at the intersections of race, nationa ity and gender. 168

intertextuality   The way in which one text echoes or refers t another. 22, 59

intonation   Tunes, created from variations in pitch, that conve meaning in the speech of a particular language. 79, 84, 103, 178

intransitive verbs   An intransitive verb does not need an object, fo example 'I slept'. 28

knowledge economy   Sometimes referred to as post-industrial econo mies. National economies that depend on knowledge-based wor rather than manual labour. 66

lexis   The vocabulary of a language. 7–8

limitations   See **communication constraints**. 181

Linguistics   The academic study of the nature of language. Ther are many branches of study including psycholinguistics (the rela tionship between language and psychology) and sociolinguistic (the relationship between language and sociology). 2, 11, 21, 38 131, 134–7

Literary Criticism   The practice of analysing works of literature. Th 'criticism' in literary criticism is different from the negative sens it has in everyday language – although literary critics may well be negative in their judgements of literary works. 'Criticism' here i more closely related to the idea of critique where evaluation and judgement are part of the process of analysis. 17, 56, 68, 112, 130–1

literature review   A discussion of various sources that are relevant to the research in question. 173–4

litotes   A rhetorical strategy whereby a speaker uses understatement for effect – for example, saying of two people in a relationship that 'they are not the happiest couple in the world'. 88

ew Englishes (Also termed 'World Englishes'.) These are varieties of English that are used in different countries around the world, mainly in areas that were formerly colonised, such as India and Singapore. These countries have their own version of standard English. 157

ominalisation The process of changing items from different word classes into nouns or noun phrases. This can have the effect of depersonalising and formalising the style of communication, and can be used to obscure agency and therefore responsibility – e.g. 'we dismissed the workers' becomes 'the dismissal of the workers', changing 'dismissed' (verb) to 'dismissal' (noun). 136

on-standard Different from mainstream usage. In language study, this label is often used for regional dialect usage, as a contrast to standard English. 142, 155–7

bserver's paradox The paradox that the only way to collect natural speech is to observe it – but the very act of observation is likely to destroy its naturalness. 176

mniscient narrator An 'all-knowing' figure who can report everything, including the thoughts inside all of the characters' heads. 132, 142

ntological metaphor A metaphor based on describing something abstract (like time) as if it were concrete (like money). 57

rally/aurally Using the communication channel of sound, via speaking and listening. 73, 83, 177

rganisational discourse Language and forms of communication that are used in, and associated with, formal organisations which direct human activity whether as places of work, worship or leisure. Organisational discourse is made up of the talk, texts, documents, objects and spaces that identify and sustain such human activity. Organisational discourse(s) intersect with many other discourses; for example, the talk and text characteristic of a hospital will heavily reference discourses of health, while managing the human resources of an organisation will involve discourses of equality and gender. 16

rientational metaphor A metaphor based on ideas about physical direction and position. 57, 66

overt prestige Status that is publicly acknowledged. 111

oxymoron A logical contradiction, for example 'a wise fool'. 167

paradigm(atic) Used specifically in Linguistics, and closely associated with Semiotics, a paradigm is a system of optional choices between items that could fill the same slot – for example, inste[ad] of referring to the noun 'war', one might refer to 'conflic[t]' 'tension' or 'trouble', each of which gives a subtly different co[n]notation about the events being described.

In social sciences, the term paradigm still means choices b[ut] in a more philosophical sense to denote the radical differenc[e] between the approaches adopted by scholars in pursuit of the[ir] studies. Contrasts might be made between positivist and interpre[-] tivist paradigms which loosely equate to the difference betwee[n] quantitative and qualitative approaches to research. 19

paralanguage Aspects of an individual's vocal expression, such [as] whispering, laughter or breathiness. 80, 178

paralipsis A rhetorical strategy whereby a speaker says they are n[ot] going to mention something, and by saying that, they mentio[n] it. 86

parallelism The use of a pair of expressions that echo each othe[r] and have some elements in common – e.g. 'tough on crime, an[d] tough on the causes of crime'. 85

pathos In the field of rhetoric, an appeal to emotion – e.g. patriot[-] ism, or appeals to family ties. 75–6

pedagogy/pedagogical The theory and practice of teaching. 45

personification Treating an object as if it were a person. 66

phatic Language that is devoid of specific content but that supports socia[l] relationships – e.g. chatting with strangers at a bus stop. 124, 129

phonetic A technical and detailed representation of speech sounds. 178

point of view The position of the narrator in relation to the story 131–4, 140

politeness An aspect of pragmatics that refers to the cultural rules o[f] a community and regulates how social relationships are negotiated 108, 123

polysyllabic Having many syllables. A syllable is a unit of organisa[-] tion in speech, normally containing a single vowel plus one o[r] more consonants. It reflects the way a word is divided into part[s] when pronounced – for example, the word 'tomato' has three syllables, to-ma-to. 19

postcolonial Academic approaches that identify and highlight the enduring legacy of European and American colonialism for con[-] temporary issues. 145, 147, 157

regional dialect grammar   Grammatical structures that are used an[d] understood by large numbers of people in particular region[s]. Examples include prepositions such as 'where's it *to*?' (Sou[th] West) and 'ten *while* twelve' (meaning ten until twelve) in som[e] parts of Yorkshire. 156

regional dialect vocabulary   Vocabulary items that are used and unde[r]stood by large numbers of people in particular regions. Example[s] include regional terms for different foodstuffs – e.g. bread rol[ls] are 'barmcakes' in some areas of the North West, 'stotties' i[n] Newcastle and 'cobs' in the Midlands. 155

register   The varieties of language use common to particular social [or] professional contexts. For example, the language used in formal an[d] institutional settings is different from that used with close friend[s]. Equally, work contexts often demand particular occupational reg[-]isters (e.g. legal, medical and therapeutic registers). 4, 20, 78, 107

reinforcements   Signals by listeners that they are happy for speake[rs] to continue – e.g. by saying 'mm'. 101

relative clause   Clauses that begin with relative pronouns – who, whic[h,] that. Relative clauses often describe or add information to the ele[-]ment that precedes them – e.g. in 'here is the book that I suggested[']' 'that I suggested' adds information to the noun 'book'. 91

relativism   A relativist view of language is that it is difficult, but sti[ll] possible, for people to think beyond the parameters of the lan[-]guage that is available to them. 25–6

representation   Something that stands in place of something else[.] Representation is how something *appears* to be, not necessaril[y] how something *is*. 26–8, 44–5, 74–5, 114, 122, 135–7, 152–3[,] 162–3, 177–8, 184

resistance narrative   Stories that go against or resist the value[s] expressed in dominant cultural narratives. 147–8

rhetoric   The art of persuasive communication, particularly in spo[-]ken texts such as formal speeches. The study of rhetoric draw[s] on rules of composition formulated by critics of ancient times[,] particularly classical Greek figures such as Aristotle. 21, 56, 68–97

rhetorical question   A question for which a speaker doesn't expect a[n] answer spoken aloud, but where an answer that agrees with the speaker is assumed – e.g. 'can it possibly be right that criminals should go unpunished?' 86–7

social identities That part of an individual's sense of themselves th maps their sense of belonging to, and difference from, wid social groupings. 3, 153

socialised The process by which individuals become integrated fully functioning members of a society by learning the custom values and attitudes considered acceptable in that society. 2 152, 164

socialism A political and economic theory that advocates for t social and democratic ownership of wealth and the means k which that wealth is produced. 166

Social Sciences A broad collection of academic areas of study (ac: demic disciplines) that focus on understanding how individua and society function. Examples of academic disciplines incluc Psychology, Sociology, Political Sciences and Anthropolog Although there is disagreement about areas of overlap, Soci Sciences are usually contrasted with the Humanities and with th Natural Sciences. 3, 10, 11, 38, 64, 108, 159

Sociology The study of society, institutions (like government, wor organisations and religions) and social groups. Sociology is als concerned with how these bodies are maintained through th collective interactions of the individuals who make them up. 2 55, 101, 108, 159

Rhetoric: when ok to lie?

Sophism A form of philosophy in Ancient Greece which focuse on the craft of fashioning arguments and persuasive texts. Ther are no surviving writings by Sophists, only by those who objecte to the philosophy. 69

sound symbolism Using sounds that suggest the thing they ar describing. 88–93

source With reference to metaphor, the idea or thing that the targe is being compared with. For example, in the expression 'love is drug', the source is 'a drug'. 60–1

spatio-temporal point of view How aspects of space and time ar described in a narrative. 133–4

Speech Act Theory A theory associated with the philosophers J.L. Austi and John Searle, arguing that language is in itself action, and not sim ply a description of it – e.g. when a person says 'I promise', they ar using language to commit themselves to something. 108–10

speech noises Sounds made during speech which are not words bu convey meaning – e.g. blowing breath out to signal effort. Such interjections do not have a conventional spelling when written down as they are not part of the formal language system. However, they can often be seen in comics and other graphic representations of speech. 103, 122

andard English A language system that acts as an agreed common language, especially for formal uses. This primarily refers to the writing system of English. 122, 155–7

ory In **Stylistics**, analysts make a distinction between story, which comprises the events or facts, and the narrative, which is how the story is told, i.e. the perspective it is told from. This can be a useful distinction but not all academic areas use it. 131

oryworld The world created by the narrative. 129, 142

tructuralist Theories that focus on the deep and enduring structures that underpin how all societies and languages work. 130

tylistics The study of style choices in texts, traditionally focused on literary works but more recently encompassing other types of text. 20–1, 29, 130–1

urface metaphors Metaphors that allow simple comparisons to be made between objects or phenomena. Surface metaphors arise out of deep metaphors. 65

ymbolic A symbol is something that stands for something else, with no logical connections between the items. 27, 38, 40, 44, 48, 51, 53, 71, 88–93, 95, 130, 152, 159, 179, 181

ynchronous Occurring together at the same time – e.g. online chat, where participants share a screen and communication happens in real time. 117–18

yntagm(atic) In language study, while a paradigm is a system of options where one item could replace another, a syntagm refers to how items are arranged and the connections between them. For example, in the sentence 'they helped themselves to eggs yesterday', 'they', 'themselves' and 'eggs' are all in the plural form; and 'helped' and 'yesterday' both reflect a past event. 'They' occurs early in the sentence because it is the grammatical subject ('doer of the action'). See **paradigm(atic)**. 19–20

target With reference to metaphor, the target is the concept you are trying to describe. For example, in the expression 'love is a drug', the target is 'love'. 60–1, 64

Temperance A movement, popular in the nineteenth century, promoting moderation in, or complete abstinence from, drinking alcohol. 93

textual intervention   An active approach to literary analysis, textu
intervention involves analysts intervening in the text they a
studying – for example, by presenting the perspective of a cha
acter who is not given much coverage in the original – to ga
insights into the original text. 18

third-person point of view   A third-person narrator is not an acti
participant in the story and therefore does not mention him/he
self in the narrative, instead using third-person pronouns ('h
'she', 'it', 'they'). 132

transcript   In language study, a way to represent speech on paper
digitally that captures many of the finer details of how the spoke
language sounded in its original form. Outside of academic field
texts are sometimes called transcripts where just the words of th
speech are included, with no particular markings. This is ofte
the case online, where, for example, political speeches are writte
out and 'tidied up' from the original version. 74, 102, 105, 178–

transgender   (Sometimes shortened to trans.) A collective term t
denote those who either reject the common gender binary
male/female or feel that this binary fails to describe their sens
of gender, or those who transition from one of these categorie
to another. As a collective term it implicates categories of se
(female/male) and gender (woman/man) as well as ideas of mas
culinity/femininity. From a transgender perspective, those wh
are not transgender are referred to as cisgender. 50–1

transitive verbs   A transitive verb needs an object, for example '
enjoyed the film'. 28

Translation Studies   The formal academic study of issues arising from
the activity of translating between languages. 31

tricolon   A list of three items in a row – e.g. 'tall, dark and handsome'
82–4, 92

trope   An example of figurative language such as a metaphor, or
frequently occurring device. The Internet 'meme' is an exampl
of a modern trope. 57, 64, 82, 144

variation analysis   An approach to language research that focuses or
how individuals vary their language from context to context, o
how groups vary in their language use. 110–11